Sao Paulo

Alex Robinson

Credits

Footprint credits
Editor: Alan Murphy
Production and layout: Patrick Dawson, Elysia Alim, Danielle Bricker
Maps: Kevin Feeney

Managing Director: Andy Riddle
Commercial Director: Patrick Dawson
Publisher: Alan Murphy
Publishing Managers: Felicity Laughton, Nicola Gibbs
Digital Editors: Jo Williams, Tom Mellors
Marketing and PR: Liz Harper
Sales: Diane McEntee
Advertising: Renu Sibal
Finance and Administration: Elizabeth Taylor

Photography credits
Front cover: Jbor/Shutterstock
Back cover: Fabio Fersa/Shutterstock

Printed and Bound in the United States of America

Every effort has been made to ensure that the facts in this guidebook are accurate. However, travellers should still obtain advice from consulates, airlines, etc about travel and visa requirements before travelling. The authors and publishers cannot accept responsibility for any loss, injury or inconvenience however caused.

Publishing information
Footprint *Focus São Paulo*
1st edition
© Footprint Handbooks Ltd
July 2011

ISBN: 978 1 908206 02 2
CIP DATA: A catalogue record for this book is available from the British Library

® Footprint Handbooks and the Footprint mark are a registered trademark of Footprint Handbooks Ltd

Published by Footprint
6 Riverside Court
Lower Bristol Road
Bath BA2 3DZ, UK
T +44 (0)1225 469141
F +44 (0)1225 469461
footprinttravelguides.com

Distributed in the USA by Globe Pequot Press, Guilford, Connecticut

All rights reserved. No part of this publication may be reproduced, stored in a retrieval system, or transmitted, in any form or by any means, electronic, mechanical, photocopying, recording, or otherwise without the prior permission of Footprint Handbooks Ltd.

The content of Footprint *Focus São Paulo* has been taken directly from Footprint's *Brazil Handbook*, which was researched and written by Alex Robinson.

Contents

5 Introduction
- 4 *Map: Region*

6 Planning your trip
- 6 Getting there
- 7 Getting around
- 8 *Map: São Paulo Metro & CPTM urban rail*
- 10 Orientation
- 10 Sleeping
- 12 Eating and drinking
- 13 Responsible travel
- 14 Essentials A-Z

20 São Paulo city
- 24 Background
- 23 *Map: São Paulo orientation*
- 25 Centro Historico
- 26 *Map: São Paulo centre & Bela Vista*
- 30 North of the centre
- 32 West of the centre
- 34 *Map: Avenida Paulista & Jardins*
- 36 South of the centre
- 39 Further afield
- 41 The suburbs
- 43 Listings

65 The Coast of São Paulo
- 66 Santos and Sao Vicente
- 67 *Map: Santos*
- 70 Litoral Norte
- 73 Ubatuba
- 74 Litoral Sul
- 78 Listings

87 Index

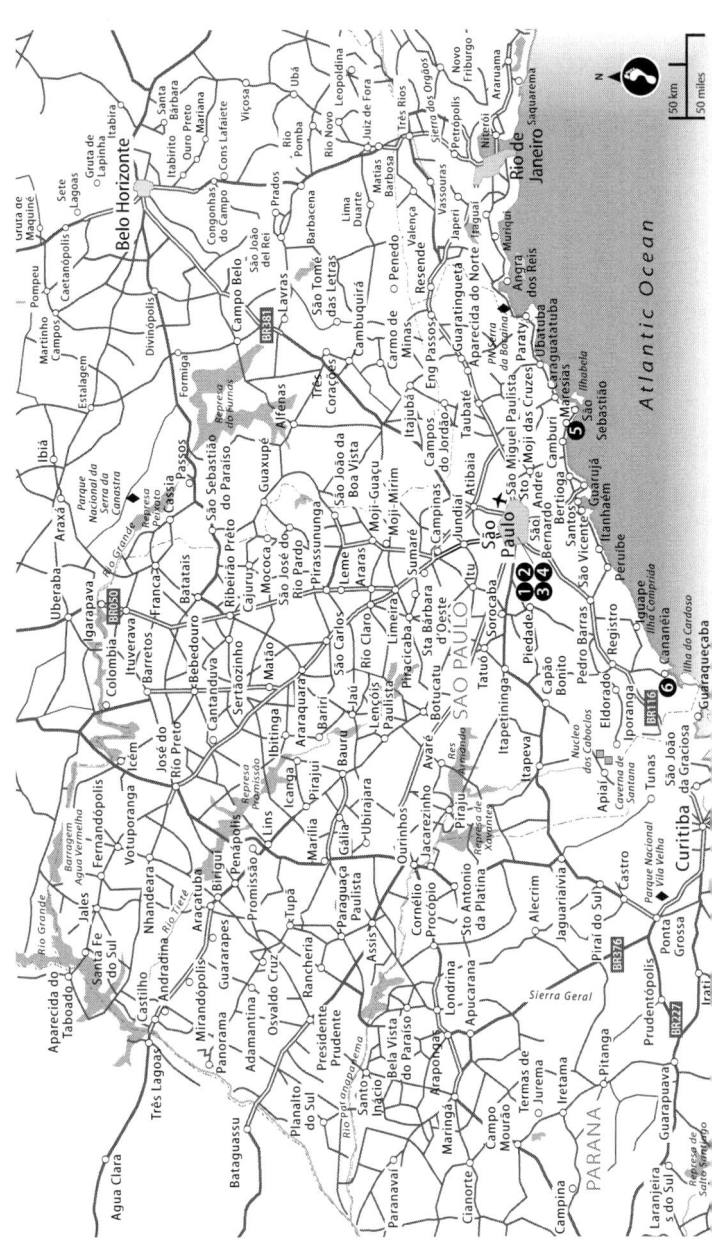

São Paulo is as famous for its ugliness as Rio is for its beauty. But while Rio looks marvellous from a distance and less than perfect close to, São Paulo is the opposite. Restaurants, shops, hotels and nightlife here are infinitely better than in Rio. And, while wandering and browsing in plush neighbourhoods such as Jardins, it is even possible to forget that few cities in the world have quite so much relentless concrete punctuated with quite so few green spaces; or have rivers quite so disgracefully polluted as the Tietê. Marlene Dietrich perhaps summed it up when she said – "Rio is a beauty – but São Paulo; ah … São Paulo is a city."

Indeed, São Paulo is more than a city. It is also a state a little larger than the UK; and while most of its interior is dull agricultural hinterland, its coast is magnificent; just as beautiful as Rio de Janeiro's but far less visited by international tourists. The northern beaches are long and glorious and pounded by some of South America's finest surf. Brazil's largest island, which is every bit as pristine and romantic as Ilha Grande, lies a short boat ride off shore. The beaches further south are less beautiful but far wilder; behind them, stretching into the neighbouring state of Paraná, are the largest expanses of primary forest on Brazil's Atlantic coast.

Don't miss ...

1 **Fine art in MASP**, page 32.
2 **Oscar Niemeyer buildings in São Paulo**, page 37.
3 **São Paulo restaurants**, page 46.
4 **São Paulo nightlife**, page 51.
5 **Beaches and waterfalls on Ihabela**, page 71.
6 **Cananéia and wild Ilha do Cardoso**, page 77.

Numbers relate to numbers on map.

Planning your trip

Getting there

Air

São Paulo is the cheapest and the principal entry point to Brazil and is one of the key entry points to South America. All international flights (except a handful to Bolivia) and many of the cheapest internal flights arrive at **Guarulhos airport** ⓘ *Guarulhos, 25 km northeast of the city, T011-2445 2945, www.infraero.gov.br*, officially known as **Cumbica**. There are plenty of banks and money changers in the arrivals hall, open daily 0800-2200, and cafés, restaurants and gift shops on the second floor and arrivals lobby. There is a post office on the third floor of Asa A. Tourist information, including city and regional city maps and copies of the entertainment section from the Folha de São Paulo newspaper with current listings, is available from **Secretaria de Esportes e Turismo (SET)** ⓘ *ground floor of both terminals, Mon-Fri 0730-2200, Sat, Sun and holidays 0900-2100*.

Airport taxis charge US$65 to the centre and operate on a ticket system: go to the second booth on leaving the terminal and book a co-op taxi at the Taxi Comum counter; these are the best value. **Guarucoop** ⓘ *T011-6440 7070, 24 hrs, www.guarucoop.com.br*, is a leading, safe radio taxi company operating from the airport. The following **Emtu buses** ⓘ *www.emtu.sp.gov.br/aeroporto*, run every 30-45 minutes (depending on the bus line) from Guarulhos between 0545 and 2215, to the following locations: **Nos 257 and 299** – Guarulhos to Metrô Tatuape (for the red line and connections to the centre), US$2; **No 258** for Congonhas airport via Avenida 23 de Maio and Avenida Rubem Berta, US$15; **No 259** for the Praça da República via Luz and Avenida Tiradentes, US$15; **No 316** for the principal hotels around Paulista and Jardins via Avenida Paulista, Rua Haddock Lobo and Rua Augusta, US$15; **No 437** for Itaím and Avenida Brigadeiro Faria Lima in the new business district, via Avenida Nove de Julho and Avenida Presidente Juscelino Kubitschek; and **No 472** for the Barra Funda Rodoviária and metrô station via the Rodoviária Tiete. A full timetable for each line with precise leaving times is listed on the website. **Airport Bus Service Pássaro Marron** ⓘ *T0800-285 3047, www.airportbusservice.com.br*, also run buses between the airport, the city centre, *rodoviária*, Congonhas airport, Avenida Paulista and Jardins hotels, Avenida Faria Lima, metrô Tatuape, *rodoviária* Tietê and the Praca da República. Buses leave every 10 minutes from 0500-0200 costing US$12.50, children under five free. All are air conditioned and a free paper and bottle of water is provided for the journey. They also run a service directly from the airport to Ubatuba and São Sebastião (for Ilhabela). Full details of this and other services are listed on their website. The company have waiting rooms in terminals 1 and 2 at Guarulhos – look for their distinctive red and blue logo or ask at the tour information desk if you can't find the lounge.

Flights with the Brazilian franchise of the US budget airline, Azul ⓘ *www.voeazul.com.br*, have begun to run from **Viracopos airport** in the city of **Campinas** just under 100 km from São Paulo, which the company cheekily calls São Paulo Campinas airport. Fares are very competitive and the company runs a bus connection between Campinas and São Paulo which connects with the flights. Azul buses leave from Terminal Barra Funda and Shopping Eldorado (Estação CPTM Hebraica Rebouças) around every 30 minutes – details on website.

The domestic airport, **Congonhas** ⓘ *Av Washington Luiz, 7 km south of the centre, 5 km from Jardins, T011-5090 9000*, is used for the Rio–São Paulo shuttle (about 400 flights a week, US$150 single, US$300 return) and some other domestic services including Salvador, Belo Horizonte and Vitória. A taxi to the city centre or Jardins costs about US$30.

Bus

There are four main bus terminals (*rodoviárias*) in São Paulo. You'll find details of bus times and prices in Portuguese at www.passagem-em-domicilio.com.br. Most buses arrive at the **Rodoviária do Tietê** ⓘ *the largest bus terminal in Latin America situated 5 km north of the centre, T011-2223 7152*. Left luggage costs US$6 per day per item. You can sleep in the bus station after 2200 after the guards leave; showers US$6. There is a metrô with connections throughout the city, US$1.20, and buses to the centre (less safe), US$0.80. Taxis to Jardins cost US$25, US$30 at weekends. Buses from the São Paulo state coast and Paraná arrive at **Barra Funda** ⓘ *T011-3666 4682*, while buses from Minas Gerais arrive at **Bresser** ⓘ *T011-6692 5191*. Buses from Santos and the coast arrive at **Jabaquara** ⓘ *T011-5581 0856*. All are connected to the centre by metrô. ▸▸ *See Transport, page 61.*

Train

Railways are being privatized and many long-distance passenger services have been withdrawn. São Paulo has four stations but the only one useful for tourists is **Estação da Luz** ⓘ *Metrô Luz, T0800-550121*, which receives trains from the northwest and southeast of São Paulo state and connects with the tourist train from Paranapiacaba to Rio Grande da Serra. See CPTM and Metrô, pages 62 and 63.

Getting around

Bus

Buses in São Paulo are operated by **SP Trans** ⓘ *www.sptrans.com.br*, who have an excellent bus route planner on their website. The system is fairly self-explanatory even for non-Portuguese speakers – with boxes allowing you to select a point of departure (*de*) and destination (*para*). It also enables you to plan using a combination of bus, metrô and urban light railway (*trem*). Google maps mark São Paulo bus stops and numbers. Right clicking on the number shows the bus route and time and there is a search facility for planning routes. There is a flat fee of US$1.20 for any bus ride – payable to a conductor sitting behind a turnstile in the bus. The conductors are helpful in indicating where to hop on and off. Buses are marked with street names indicating their routes, but these routes can be confusing for visitors and services slow due to frequent traffic jams. However, buses are safe, clean and only crowded at peak hours (0700-0900 and 1700-1830). Maps of the bus and metrô system are available at depots, eg Anhangabaú.

Metrô and the CPTM Urban light railway

The best and cheapest way to get around São Paulo is on the excellent **metrô system** ⓘ *daily 0500-2400, www.metro.sp.gov.br, with a clear journey planner and information in Portuguese and English*, which is clean, safe, cheap and efficient. It is integrated with the overground CPTM light railway. São Paulo's was the first metrô in Brazil, beginning operations in 1975. It now has five main lines.

The CPTM (Companhia Paulista de Trens Metropolitanos) ⓘ *www.cptm.sp.gov.br*, is an urban light railway which serves to extend the metrô along the margins of the Tietê and Pinheiros rivers and to the outer city suburbs. There are six lines, which are colour-coded like the metrô. ▸ *For details, see Transport, page 62.*

São Paulo Metro & CPTM urban rail

▬ ▬ ▬ ▬ ▬ Due for completion 2011-2014

Taxi

Taxis in São Paulo are white with a green light on the roof. They display their tariffs in the window (starting at US$5) and have meters. Ordinary taxis are hailed on the street or more safely at taxi stations (*postos*), which are never more than five minute's walk away

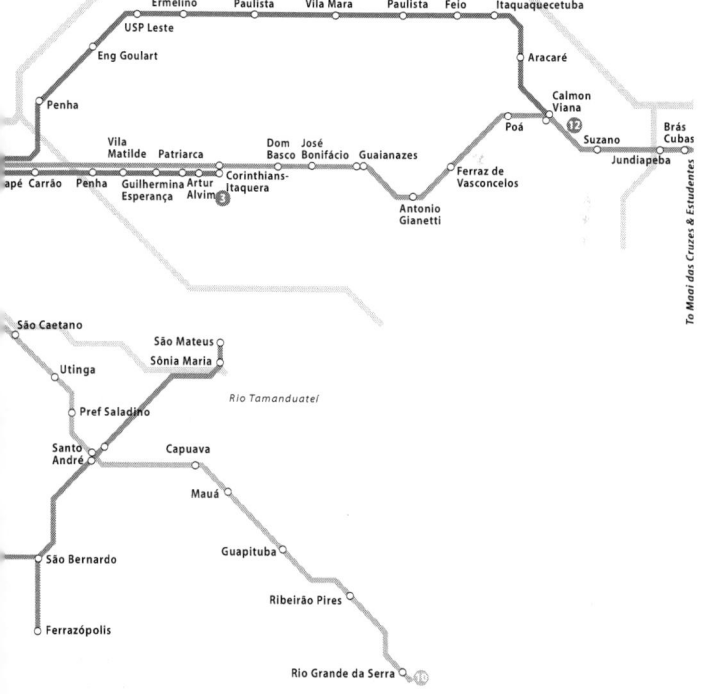

anywhere in the city. Hotels, restaurants and some venues will call a taxi on request – either from a *posto* or a taxi driver himself. Radio taxis are more expensive but less hassle.
▸▸ *See Transport, page 63, for recommended companies.*

Sleeping

There is a good range of accommodation options in Brazil. An *albergue* or hostel offers the cheapest option. These have dormitory beds and single and double rooms. Many are part of the IYHA, www.iyha.org. Hostel world, www.hostelworld.com; Hostel Bookers, www.hostelbookers.com; and Hostel.com, www.hostel.com, are useful portals. Hostel Trail Latin America – T0131-208 0007 (UK), www.hosteltrail.com – managed from their hostel in Popayan, is an online network of hotels and tour companies in South America. A *pensão* is either a cheap guesthouse or a household that rents out some rooms.

A *pousada* is either a bed-and-breakfast, often small and family-run, or a sophisticated and often charming small hotel. A *hotel* is as it is anywhere else in the world, operating according to the international star system, although five-star hotels are not price controlled and hotels in any category are not always of the standard of their star equivalent in the USA, Canada or Europe. Many of the older hotels can be cheaper than hostels. Usually accommodation prices include a breakfast of rolls, ham, cheese, cakes and fruit with coffee and juice; there is no reduction if you don't eat it. Rooms vary too. Normally an *apartamento* is a room with separate living and sleeping areas and sometimes cooking facilities. A *quarto* is a standard room; *com banheiro* is en suite; and *sem banheiro* is with shared bathroom. Finally there are the *motels*. These should not be confused with their US counterpart: motels are used by guests not intending to sleep; there is no stigma attached and they usually offer good value (the rate for a full night is called the '*pernoite*'), however the decor can be a little garish.

It's a good idea to book accommodation in advance in small towns that are popular at weekends with city dwellers (eg near São Paulo and Rio de Janeiro), and it's essential to book at peak times.

Luxury accommodation

Much of the luxury private accommodation sector can be booked through operators. Angatu, www.angatu.com, offers the best private homes along the Costa Verde, together with bespoke trips. Dehouche, www.dehouche.com, offers upmarket accommodation and trips in Bahia, Rio and Alagoas. Brazilian Beach House, www.brazilianbeachhouse.com, has some of the finest houses in Búzios and Trancoso but is not so great at organizing transfers and pick-ups. Matuete, www.matuete.com, has a range of luxurious properties and tours throughout Brazil.

Camping

Those with an international camping card pay only half the rate of a non-member at Camping Clube do Brasil sites, www.campingclube.com.br. Membership of the club itself is expensive: US$85 for six months. The club has 43 sites in 13 states and 80,000 members. It may be difficult to get into some Camping Clube campsites during high season (January to February). Private campsites charge about US$8-15 per person. For those on a very low budget and in isolated areas where there is no campsite available, it's usually possible to stay at service stations. They have shower facilities, watchmen and food; some have dormitories. There are

Sleeping and eating price codes

Sleeping

$$$$	over US$150	**$$$**	US$66-150
$$	US$30-65	**$**	Under US$30

Prices include taxes and service charge, but not meals. They are based on a double room, except in the **$** range, where prices are almost always per person.

Eating

🍴🍴🍴 Expensive over US$12   🍴🍴 Mid-range US$6-12
🍴 Cheap under US$6

Prices refer to the cost of a two-course meal, not including drinks.

---

also various municipal sites. Campsites tend to be some distance from public transport routes and are better suited to people with their own car. Wild camping is generally difficult and dangerous. Never camp at the side of a road; this is very risky.

Homestays

Staying with a local family is an excellent way to become integrated quickly into a city and companies try to match guests to their hosts. Cama e Café, www.camaecafe.com.br, organizes homestays in Rio de Janeiro, Olinda and a number of other cities around Brazil. Couch surfing, www.couchsurfing.com, offers a free, backpacker alternative.

Quality hotel associations

The better international hotel associations have members in Brazil. These include: **Small Luxury Hotels of the World**, www.slh.com; the **Leading Hotels of the World**, www.lhw.com; the **Leading Small Hotels of the World**, www.leadingsmallhotels oftheworld.com; **Great Small Hotels**, www.greatsmallhotels.com; and the **French Relais et Chateaux group**, www.relaischateaux.com, which also includes restaurants.

The Brazilian equivalent of these associations is the **Roteiros de Charme**, www.roteiros decharme.com.br, with some 30 locations in the southeast and northeast. Whilst membership of these groups pretty much guarantees quality, it is by no means comprehensive. There are many fine hotels and charming *pousadas* listed in our text that are not included in these associations.

Online travel agencies (OTAs)

Services like **Tripadvisor** and OTAs associated with them – such as **hotels.com**, **expedia.com** and **venere.com**, are well worth using for both reviews and for booking ahead. Hotels booked through an OTA can be up to 50% cheaper than the rack rate. Similar sites operate for hostels (though discounts are far less considerable). They include the **Hostelling International** site, www.hihostels.com, **hostelbookers.com**, **hostels.com** and **hostelworld.com**.

Eating and drinking

Food
Brazilians consider their cuisine to be up there with the world's best. Visitors may disagree. Mains are generally heavy, meaty and unspiced. Deserts are often very sweet. That said, the best cooking south of the Rio Grande is in São Paulo and Rio, where a heady mix of international immigrants has resulted in some unusual fusion cooking and exquisite variations on French, Japanese, Portuguese, Arabic and Italian traditional techniques and dishes. The regional cooking in Pará is also a delight – utilizing unusual and unique fruits and vegetables from the Amazon and the sumptuous Amazonian river fish.

Outside the more sophisticated cities it can be a struggle to find interesting food. The Brazilian staple meal generally consists of a cut of fried or barbecued meat, chicken or fish accompanied by rice, black or South American broad beans and an unseasoned salad of lettuce, grated carrot, tomato and beetroot. Condiments are weak chilli sauce, olive oil, salt and pepper and vinegar.

The national dish is a greasy campfire stew called *feijoada*, made by throwing jerked beef, smoked sausage, tongue and salt pork into a pot with lots of fat and beans and stewing it for hours. The resulting stew is sprinkled with fried *farofa* (manioc flour) and served with *couve* (kale) and slices of orange. The meal is washed down with *cachaça* (sugarcane rum). Most restaurants serve the *feijoada completa* for Saturday lunch (up until about 1630). Come with a very empty stomach.

Brazil's other national dish is mixed grilled meat or *churrasco*, served in vast portions off the spit by legions of rushing waiters, and accompanied by a buffet of salads, beans and mashed vegetables. *Churrascos* are served in *churrascarias* or *rodízios*. The meat is generally excellent, especially in the best *churascarias*, and the portions are unlimited, offering good value for camel-stomached carnivores able to eat one meal a day.

In remembrance of Portugal, but bizarrely for a tropical country replete with fish, Brazil is the world's largest consumer of **cod**, pulled from the cold north Atlantic, salted and served in watery slabs or little balls as *bacalhau* (an appetizer/bar snack) or *petisco*. Other national *petiscos* include *kibe* (a deep-fried or baked mince with onion, mint and flour), *coxinha* (deep-fried chicken or meat in dough), *empadas* (baked puff-pastry patties with prawns, chicken, heart of palm or meat), and *tortas* (little pies with the same ingredients). When served in bakeries, *padarias* or snack bars these are collectively referred to as *salgadinhos* (savouries).

Eating cheaply
The cheapest dish is the *prato feito* or *sortido*, an excellent-value set menu usually comprising meat/chicken/fish, beans, rice, chips and salad. The *prato comercial* is similar but rather better and a bit more expensive. Portions are usually large enough for two and come with two plates. If you are on your own, you could ask for an *embalagem* (doggy bag) or a *marmita* (takeaway) and offer it to a person with no food (many Brazilians do). Many restaurants serve *comida por kilo* buffets where you serve yourself and pay for the weight of food on your plate. This is generally good value and is a good option for vegetarians. *Lanchonetes* and *padarias* (diners and bakeries) are good for cheap eats; usually serving *prato feitos*, *salgadinhos*, excellent juices and other snacks.

The main meal is usually taken in the middle of the day; cheap restaurants tend not to be open in the evening.

Drink

The national liquor is *cachaça* (also known as *pinga*), which is made from sugar-cane, and ranging from cheap supermarket and service-station fire-water, to boutique distillery and connoisseur labels from the interior of Minas Gerais. Mixed with fruit juice, sugar and crushed ice, *cachaça* becomes the principal element in a *batida*, a refreshing but deceptively powerful drink. Served with pulped lime or other fruit, mountains of sugar and smashed ice it becomes the world's favourite party cocktail, caipirinha. A less potent caipirinha made with vodka is called a *caipiroska* and with sake a *saikirinha* or *caipisake*.

Brazilian beer is generally lager, served ice-cold. Draught beer is called *chope* or *chopp* (after the German Schoppen, and pronounced 'shoppi'). There are various national brands of bottled beers, which include Brahma, Skol, Cerpa, Antartica and the best Itaipava and Bohemia. There are black beers too, notably Xingu. They tend to be sweet. The best beer is from the German breweries in Rio Grande do Sul and is available only there.

Brazil's myriad fruits are used to make fruit juices or *sucos*, which come in a delicious variety, unrivalled anywhere in the world. *Açai, acerola, caju* (cashew), *pitanga, goiaba* (guava), *genipapo, graviola* (chirimoya), *maracujá* (passion fruit), *sapoti, umbu* and *tamarindo* are a few of the best. *Vitaminas* are thick fruit or vegetable drinks with milk. *Caldo de cana* is sugar-cane juice, sometimes mixed with ice. *Água de côco* or *côco verde* is coconut water served straight from a chilled, fresh, green coconut. The best known of many local soft drinks is *guaraná*, which is a very popular carbonated fruit drink, completely unrelated to the Amazon nut. The best variety is *guaraná Antarctica*. Coffee is ubiquitous and good tea entirely absent.

Responsible travel

Sustainable or ecotourism is not just about looking after the physical environment, but also the local community. Whilst it has been slow to catch up with Costa Rica or Ecuador, Brazil now has some first-rate ecotourism projects and the country is a pioneer in urban community tourism in the favelas. Model ecotourism resorts in the forest include **Pousada Uacari** and **Cristalino Jungle Lodge**. **Fazenda San Francisco** in the Pantanal runs a pioneering jaguar conservation project; **REGUA** and **Serra dos Tucanos** on the Atlantic coast have done a great deal to protect important birding habitats; and resorts such as **Mata N'ativa** in Trancoso are taking important first steps in beach holiday areas. In the Amazon, Atlantic coast forest and parts of the *cerrado*, access to certain wilderness areas is restricted to scientists. Having such a low-impact policy over these regions means that their environment is protected from damage or over-use. In much of coastal Brazil, where tourism and property speculation has boomed in the last few years, the impact on local communities is particularly devastating. Some state governments cheerfully exploit the colourful local culture while sharing little of the profit. So rather than staying in a big resort and organizing a tour from back home, seek out smaller locally owned hotels and local indigenous guides. Try to visit projects such as the **Pataxó Reserve** in Jaqueira, Porto Seguro, and support the Caiçaras near Paraty.

Essentials A-Z

Accident and emergency
Ambulance T192. **Police** T190. If robbed or attacked, contact the tourist police. If you need to claim on insurance, make sure you get a police report.

Electricity
Generally 110 V 60 cycles AC, but in some cities and areas 220 V 60 cycles AC is used. European and U.S 2-pin plugs and sockets.

Embassies and consulates
For embassies and consulates of Brazil, see www.embassiesabroad.com.

Health → *Hospitals/medical services are listed in the Directory sections.*
See your GP or travel clinic at least 6 weeks before departure for general advice on travel risks and vaccinations. Try phoning a specialist travel clinic if your own doctor is unfamiliar with health in the region. Make sure you have sufficient medical travel insurance, get a dental check, know your own blood group and, if you suffer a long-term condition such as diabetes or epilepsy, obtain a **Medic Alert** bracelet (www.medicalalert.co.uk).

Vaccinations and anti-malarials
Confirm that your primary courses and boosters are up to date. It is advisable to vaccinate against polio, tetanus, typhoid, hepatitis A and, for more remote areas, rabies. Yellow fever vaccination is obligatory for most areas. Cholera, diptheria and hepatitis B vaccinations are sometimes advised. Specialist advice should be taken on the best antimalarials to take before you leave.

Health risks
The major risks posed in the region are those caused by insect disease carriers such as mosquitoes and sandflies. The key parasitic and viral diseases are malaria, South American trypanosomiasis (Chagas disease) and dengue fever. Be aware that you are always at risk from these diseases. **Malaria** is a danger throughout the lowland tropics and coastal regions. **Dengue fever** (which is currently rife in Rio de Janeiro state) is particularly hard to protect against as the mosquitoes can bite throughout the day as well as night (unlike those that carry malaria); try to wear clothes that cover arms and legs and also use effective mosquito repellent. Mosquito nets dipped in permethrin provide a good physical and chemical barrier at night. **Chagas disease** is spread by faeces of the triatomine, or assassin bugs, whereas sandflies spread a disease of the skin called **leishmaniasis**.

Some form of **diarrhoea** or intestinal upset is almost inevitable, the standard advice is always to wash your hands before eating and to be careful with drinking water and ice; if you have any doubts about the water then boil it or filter and treat it. In a restaurant buy bottled water or ask where the water has come from. Food can also pose a problem, be wary of salads if you don't know whether they have been washed or not.

There is a constant threat of **tuberculosis** (TB) and although the BCG vaccine is available, it is still not guaranteed protection. It is best to avoid unpasteurized dairy products and try not to let people cough and splutter all over you.

Another risk, especially to campers and people with small children, is that of the **hanta virus**, which is carried by some forest and riverine rodents. Symptoms are a flu-like illness which can lead to complications. Try as far as possible to avoid rodent-infested areas, especially close contact with rodent droppings.

Money
Currency
➔ *£1 = 2.65; €1 = R$2.38; US$1 = R$1.6 (May 2011)*. The unit of currency is the **real**, R$ (plural **reais**). Any amount of foreign currency and 'a reasonable sum' in reais can be taken in, but sums over US$10,000 must be declared. Residents may only take out the equivalent of US$4000. Notes in circulation are: 100, 50, 10, 5 and 1 real; coins: 1 real, 50, 25, 10, 5 and 1 centavo. **Note** The exchange- rate fluctuates – check regularly.

Costs of travelling
Brazil is more expensive than other countries in South America. As a very rough guide, prices are about two-thirds those of Western Europe and a little cheaper than rural USA; though prices vary hugely according to the current exchange rate and strength of the real, whose value has soared since 2008 – with Goldman Sachs and Bloomberg considering the *real* to be the most over-valued major currency in the world in 2009-2010. It is expected to lose value; check on the latest before leaving on currency exchange sites such as www.x-rates.com.

Hostel beds are usually around US$15. Budget hotels with few frills have rooms for as little as US$30, and you should have no difficulty finding a double room costing US$45 wherever you are. Rooms are often pretty much the same price whether 1 or 2 people are staying. Eating is generally inexpensive, especially in *padarias* or *comida por kilo* (pay by weight) restaurants, which offer a wide range of food (salads, meat, pasta, vegetarian). Expect to pay around US$6 to eat your fill in a good-value restaurant. Although bus travel is cheap by US or European standards, because of the long distances, costs can soon mount up. Internal flights prices have come down dramatically in the last couple of years and some routes work out cheaper than taking a bus – especially if booking through the internet. Prices vary regionally. Ipanema is almost twice as expensive as rural Bahia. A can of beer in a supermarket in the southeast costs US$0.80, a litre of water US$0.60, a single metrô ticket in São Paulo US$1.60, a bus ticket between US$1 and US$1.50 (depending on the city) and a cinema ticket around US$3.60.

ATMs
ATMs, or cash machines, are common in Brazil. As well as being the most convenient way of withdrawing money, they frequently offer the best available rates of exchange. They are usually closed after 2130 in large cities. There are 2 international ATM acceptance systems, **Plus** and **Cirrus**. Many issuers of debit and credit cards are linked to one, or both (eg Visa is Plus, MasterCard is Cirrus). **Bradesco** and **HSBC** are the 2 main banks offering this service. **Red Banco 24 Horas** kiosks advertise that they take a long list of credit cards in their ATMs, including MasterCard and Amex, but international cards cannot always be used; the same is true of **Banco do Brasil**.

Advise your bank before leaving, as cards are usually stopped in Brazil without prior warning. Find out before you leave what international functionality your card has. Check if your bank or credit card company imposes handling charges. Internet banking is useful for monitoring your account or transferring funds. Do not rely on 1 card, in case of loss. If you do lose a card, immediately contact the 24-hr helpline of the issuer in your home country (keep this number in a safe place).

Exchange
Banks in major cities will change cash and traveller's cheques (TCs). If you keep the official exchange slips, you may convert back into foreign currency up to 50% of the amount you exchanged. The parallel market, found in travel agencies, exchange houses

and among hotel staff, often offers marginally better rates than the banks but commissions can be very high. Many banks may only change US$300 minimum in cash, US$500 in TCs. Rates for TCs are usually far lower than for cash, they are harder to change and a very heavy commission may be charged. Dollars cash (take US$5 or US$10 bills) are not useful as alternative currency. Brazilians use *reais*.

Credit cards

Credit cards are widely used, athough often they are not usable in the most unlikely of places, such as tour operators. **Diners Club**, **MasterCard**, **Visa** and **Amex** are useful. Cash advances on credit cards will only be paid in *reais* at the tourist rate, incurring at least a 1.5% commission. Banks in small, remote places may still refuse to give a cash advance: try asking for the *gerente* (manager).

Opening hours

Generally Mon-Fri 0900-1800; closed for lunch some time between 1130 and 1400.
Shops Also open on Sat until 1230 or 1300.
Government offices Mon-Fri 1100-1800.
Banks Mon-Fri 1000-1600 or 1630; closed at weekends.

Safety

Although Brazil's big cities suffer high rates of violent crime, this is mostly confined to the favelas (slums) where poverty and drugs are the main cause. Visitors should not enter favelas except when accompanied by workers for NGOs, tour groups or other people who know the local residents well and are accepted by the community. Otherwise they may be targets of muggings by armed gangs who show short shrift to those who resist them. Mugging can take place anywhere. Travel light after dark with few valuables (avoid wearing jewellery and use a cheap, plastic, digital watch). Ask hotel staff where is and isn't safe; crime is patchy in Brazilian cities.

If the worst does happen and you are threatened, don't panic, and hand over your valuables. Do not resist, and report the crime to the local tourist police later. It is extremely rare for a tourist to be hurt during a robbery in Brazil. Being aware of the dangers, acting confidently and using your common sense will reduce many of the risks.

Photocopy your passport, air ticket and other documents, make a record of traveller's cheque and credit card numbers. Keep them separately from the originals and leave another set of records at home. Keep all documents secure; hide your main cash supply in different places or under your clothes. Extra pockets sewn inside shirts and trousers, money belts (best worn below the waist), neck or leg pouches and elasticated support bandages for keeping money above the elbow or below the knee have been repeatedly recommended.

All border areas should be regarded with some caution because of smuggling activities. Violence over land ownership in parts of the interior have resulted in a 'Wild West' atmosphere in some towns, which should therefore be passed through quickly. Red-light districts should also be given a wide berth as there are reports of drinks being drugged with a substance popularly known as 'good night Cinderella'. This leaves the victim easily amenable to having their possessions stolen, or worse.

Avoiding cons

Never trust anyone telling sob stories or offering 'safe rooms', and when looking for a hotel, always choose the room yourself. Be wary of 'plain-clothes policemen'; insist on seeing identification and on going to the police station by main roads. Do not hand over your identification (or money) until you are at the station. On no account take them directly back to your hotel. Be even more suspicious if they seek confirmation of their status from a passer-by.

Hotel security

Hotel safe deposits are generally, but not always, secure. If you cannot get a receipt for valuables in a hotel safe, you can seal the contents in a plastic bag and sign across the seal. Always keep an inventory of what you have deposited. If you don't trust the hotel, lock everything in your pack and secure it in your room when you go out. If you lose valuables, report to the police and note details of the report for insurance purposes. Be sure to be present whenever your credit card is used.

Police

There are several types of police: **Polícia Federal**, civilian dressed, who handle all federal law duties, including immigration. A subdivision is the **Polícia Federal Rodoviária**, uniformed, who are the traffic police on federal highways. **Polícia Militar** are the uniformed, street police force, under the control of the state governor, handling all state laws. They are not the same as the Armed Forces' internal police. **Polícia Civil**, also state controlled, handle local laws and investigations. They are usually in civilian dress, unless in the traffic division. In cities, the **Prefeitura** controls the **Guarda Municipal**, who handle security. **Tourist police** operate in places with a strong tourist presence. In case of difficulty, visitors should seek out tourist police in the first instance.

Public transport

When you have all your luggage with you at a bus or railway station, be especially careful and carry any shoulder bags in front of you. To be extra safe, take a taxi between the airport/bus station/railway station and hotel, keep your bags with you and pay only when you and your luggage are outside; avoid night buses and arriving at your destination at night.

Sexual assault

If you are the victim of a sexual assault, you are advised firstly to contact a doctor (this can be your home doctor). You will need tests to determine whether you have contracted any STDs; you may also need advice on emergency contraception. You should contact your embassy, where consular staff will be very willing to help.

Time

Brazil has 4 time zones: Brazilian standard time is GMT-3; the Amazon time zone (Pará west of the Rio Xingu, Amazonas, Roraima, Rondônia, Mato Grosso and Mato Grosso do Sul) is GMT-4, the State of Acre is GMT-5; and the Fernando de Noronha archipelago is GMT-2. Clocks move forward 1 hr in summer for approximately 5 months (usually between Oct and Feb or Mar), but times of change vary. This does not apply to Acre.

Tipping

Tipping is not usual, but always appreciated as staff are often paid a pittance. In restaurants, add 10% of the bill if no service charge is included; cloakroom attendants deserve a small tip; porters have fixed charges but often receive tips as well; unofficial car parkers on city streets should be tipped 2 reais.

Tourist information

The **Ministério do Turismo**, Esplanada dos Ministérios, Bloco U, 2nd and 3rd floors, Brasília, www.turismo.gov.br or www.brazil tour.com, is in charge of tourism in Brazil and has information in many languages. **Embratur**, the Brazilian Institute of Tourism, is at the same address, and is in charge of promoting tourism abroad. For information and phone numbers for your country visit www.braziltour.com. Local tourist information bureaux are not usually helpful for information on cheap hotels – they generally just dish out pamphlets. Expensive hotels provide tourist magazines for their guests. Telephone directories (not Rio) contain good street maps.

Visas and immigration

Visas are not required for stays of up to 90 days by tourists from Andorra, Argentina, Austria, Bahamas, Barbados, Belgium, Bolivia, Chile, Colombia, Costa Rica, Denmark, Ecuador, Finland, France, Germany, Greece, Iceland, Ireland, Italy, Liechtenstein, Luxembourg, Malaysia, Monaco, Morocco, Namibia, the Netherlands, Norway, Paraguay, Peru, Philippines, Portugal, San Marino, South Africa, Spain, Suriname, Sweden, Switzerland, Thailand, Trinidad and Tobago, United Kingdom, Uruguay, the Vatican and Venezuela. For them, only the following documents are required at the port of disembarkation: a passport valid for at least 6 months (or *cédula de identidad* for nationals of Argentina, Chile, Paraguay and Uruguay); and a return or onward ticket, or adequate proof that you can purchase your return fare, subject to no remuneration being received in Brazil and no legally binding or contractual documents being signed. Venezuelan passport holders can stay for 60 days on filling in a form at the border.

Citizens of the USA, Canada, Australia, New Zealand and other countries not mentioned above, and anyone wanting to stay longer than 180 days, *must* get a visa before arrival, which may, if you ask, be granted for multiple entry. US citizens must be fingerprinted on entry to Brazil. Visa fees vary from country to country, so apply to the Brazilian consulate in your home country. The consular fee in the USA is US$55. Students planning to study in Brazil or employees of foreign companies can apply for a 1- or 2-year visa. 2 copies of the application form, 2 photos, a letter from the sponsoring company or educational institution in Brazil, a police form showing no criminal convictions and a fee of around US$80 is required.

Weights and measures
Metric.

Contents

20 São Paulo city

- 21 Ins and outs
- 23 *Map: São Paulo orientation*
- 24 Background
- 25 Centro Histórico
- 26 *Map: São Paulo centre & Bela Vista*
- 30 North of the centre
- 32 West of the centre
- 34 *Map: Avenida Paulista & Jardins*
- 36 South of the centre
- 39 Further afield
- 41 The suburbs
- 43 Listings

65 The coast of São Paulo

- 66 Santos and São Vicente
- 67 *Map: Santos*
- 70 Litoral Norte
- 73 Ubatuba
- 74 Litoral Sul
- 78 Listings

Footprint features

- 21 Arriving late at night
- 63 O Bilhete Único
- 69 Great Burnt Island
- 83 The biggest rodeo in the world

São Paulo city

São Paulo is vast and can feel intimidating on first arrival. But this is a city of separate neighbourhoods, only a few of which are interesting for visitors, and once you have your base it is easy to navigate. São Paulo is the intellectual capital of Brazil. Those who don't flinch at the city's size and leave, who are instead prepared to spend time (and money) here, and who get to know Paulistanos, are seldom disappointed and often end up preferring the city to Rio. Nowhere in Brazil is better for concerts, clubs, theatre, ballet, classical music, all-round nightlife, restaurants and beautifully designed hotels. You will not be seen as a gringo in São Paulo, and the city is safer than Rio if you avoid the centre after dark and the outlying favelas (which are impossible to stumble across).

➤ *For listings, see pages 43-64.*

Ins and outs → *Phone code: 011. Population: 18-20 million. Altitude: 850 m.*

Orientation

At the heart of the city, the **Centro Histórico** is a place to visit but not to stay. Most of the historical buildings and former beauty are long gone, but its pedestrianized streets are fascinating and gritty, with lively markets and a cluster of interesting sights lost in the concrete and cobbles. For a birds' eye view of the city, head to the lookout platform at the top of the **Edifício Italia** tower, preferably at dusk. The commercial district, containing banks, offices and shops, is known as the **Triângulo**, bounded by Ruas Direita, 15 de Novembro, São Bento and Praça Antônio Prado, but it is rapidly spreading towards the Praça da República.

Immediately southwest of the Centro Histórico is the city's grandest and most photo- graphed skyscraper-lined street, **Avenida Paulista**. The Museo de Arte de São Paulo (MASP), the best art gallery in the southern hemisphere, is here. North of Avenida Paulista is the neighbourhood of **Consolação**, centred on tawdry Rua Augusta but undergoing a Renaissance at the cutting edge of the city's underground live music and nightlife scene. South of Avenida Paulista is the neighbourhood of **Jardins**. This is the city's most affluent inner neighbourhood with elegant little streets hiding Latin America's best restaurants and designer clothing boutiques. There are plenty of luxurious hotels and some budget options.

Next to Jardins, 5 km south of the centre, the **Parque do Ibirapuera** is the inner city's largest green space, with running tracks, a lake and live concerts. Like Brasília, it is a repository of historically important Oscar Niemeyer buildings, many of which are home to interesting museums. The adjoining neighbourhoods of **Vila Mariana** and **Paraíso** have a few hotel options and great live music at SESC Vila Mariana.

Situated between Ibirapuera and the river, **Itaim**, **Moema** and **Vila Olímpia** are among the nightlife centres of São Paulo with a wealth of streetside bars, ultra-chic designer restaurants and European-style dance clubs. Hotels tend to be expensive as these areas border the new business centre on Avenida Brigadeiro Faria Lima and Avenida Luís Carlos Berrini, in the suburb of **Brooklin**. **Pinheiros and Vila Madalena** are less chic, but equally lively at night and with the funkiest shops.

Arriving late at night

São Paulo's international airport, Cumbica in Guarulhos, has 24-hour facilities (for food, banking and of course taxis) in case you arrive late at night or in the early hours of the morning. It is a long drive from the airport to the city and the a/c bus to Praça da República does not operate between 0200 and 0500 and the service to Avenida Paulista does not run from 2315 to 0645. A taxi to the centre of the city will cost around US$65.

Congonhas airport, which is connected to most of Brazil's major cities, is in the city centre. Although there are no 24-hour services there are hotels across the road from the terminal (via the footbridge) and most areas in and around the centre are a maximum of US$30 taxi ride away.

São Paulo

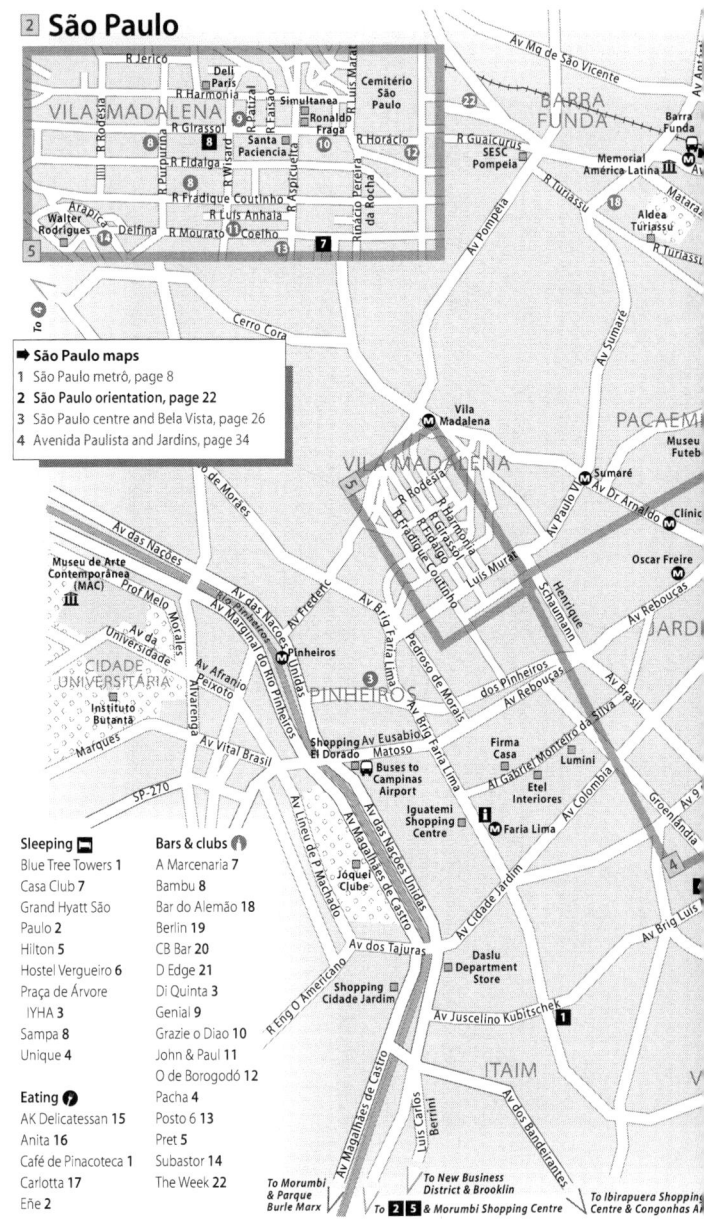

São Paulo maps
1 São Paulo metrô, page 8
2 São Paulo orientation, page 22
3 São Paulo centre and Bela Vista, page 26
4 Avenida Paulista and Jardins, page 34

Sleeping
Blue Tree Towers 1
Casa Club 7
Grand Hyatt São Paulo 2
Hilton 5
Hostel Vergueiro 6
Praça de Árvore IYHA 3
Sampa 8
Unique 4

Eating
AK Delicatessan 15
Anita 16
Café de Pinacoteca 1
Carlotta 17
Eñe 2

Bars & clubs
A Marcenaria 7
Bambu 8
Bar do Alemão 18
Berlin 19
CB Bar 20
D Edge 21
Di Quinta 3
Genial 9
Grazie o Diao 10
John & Paul 11
O de Borogodó 12
Pacha 4
Posto 6 13
Pret 5
Subastor 14
The Week 22

22 • São Paulo Ins & outs

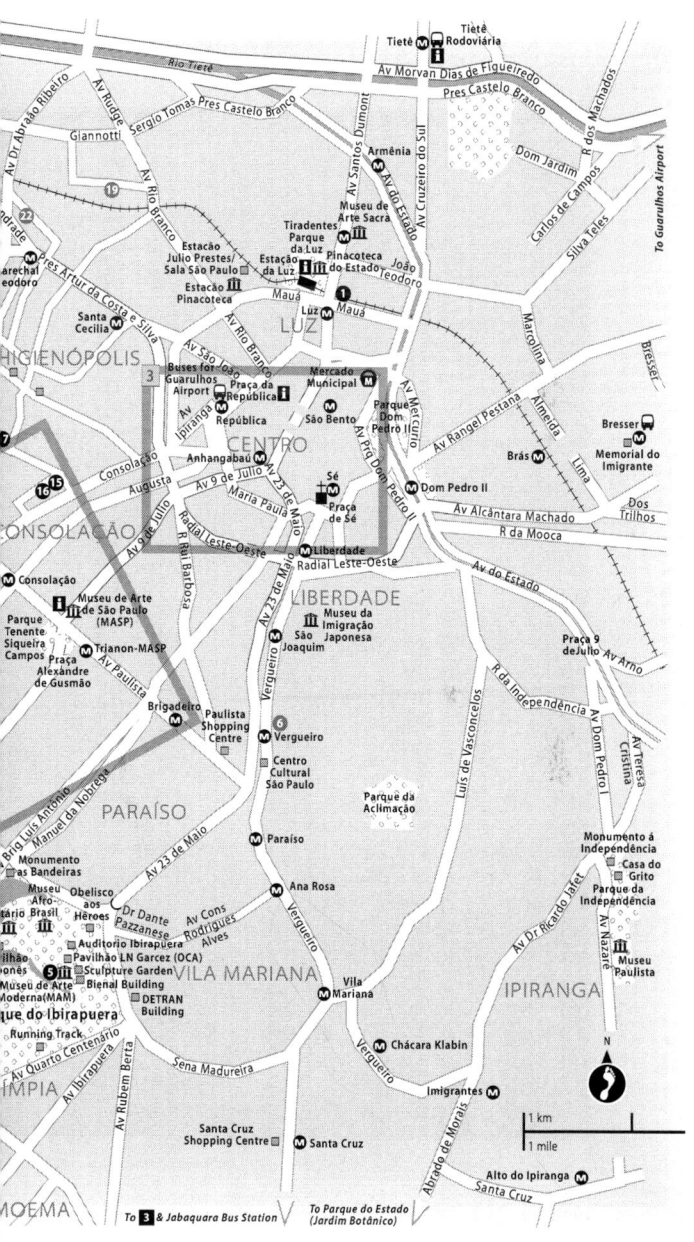

Tourist information
There are tourist information booths with English-speaking staff in international and domestic arrivals (ground floor) at **Cumbica airport** (Guarulhos). There are also tourist information booths in the **bus station** and in the following locations throughout the city: **Praça da Luz** ⓘ *in front of the Pinacoteca cafe, daily 0900-1800*; **Avenida São João** ⓘ *Av São João 473, Mon-Fri 0900-1800*; **Avenida Paulista** ⓘ *Parque Trianon, T011-3251 0970, Sun-Fri 0900-1800*; and **Avenida Brig Faria Lima** ⓘ *opposite the Iguatemi shopping centre, T011- 3211 1277, Mon-Fri 0900-1800*. An excellent map is available free at these offices.

Editora Abril publishes maps and the excellent *Guia de São Paulo – Sampa* guide (in Portuguese only). For cheap travel, *Viajar Bem e Barato*, is available at news-stands and bookshops throughout the city.

Websites The best website in English is www.brazilmax.com. www.guiasp.com.br has comprehensive entertainment listings in Portuguese, but is readily understandable. Also see http://vejasaopaulo.abril.com.br for entertainment, restaurants and general information in Portuguese.

Background

The history of São Paulo state and São Paulo city were much the same from the arrival of the Europeans until the coffee boom transformed the region's economic and political landscape. According to John Hemming in his book *Red Gold*, there were approximately 196,000 indigenous inhabitants living in what is now São Paulo state at the time of conquest. Today their numbers have been vastly diminished and of the few who survived, some live in villages within São Paulo itself and can be seen selling handicrafts in the centre.

The first official settlement in the state was at São Vicente on the coast, near today's port of Santos. It was founded in 1532 by Martim Afonso de Sousa, who had been sent by King João III to drive the French from Brazilian waters, explore the coast and lay claim to all the lands apportioned to Portugal under the Treaty of Tordesillas.

In 1554, two Jesuit priests from São Vicente founded São Paulo as a *colégio* (a combined mission and school) on the site of the present Pátio de Colégio in the Centro Histórico. The Jesuits chose to settle inland because they wanted to distance themselves from the civil authority, which was based in Bahia and along the coast. Moreover, the plateau provided better access to the indigenous population who they hoped to convert to Catholicism. Pioneers seeking to found farms followed in the Jesuits' wake and as the need for workers on these farms grew, expeditions were sent into the interior of the country to capture and enslave the indigenous people. These marauders were known as *bandeirantes* after the flag wielder who ostensibly walked at their head to claim territory. Most of their number were the culturally disenfranchised offspring of the indigenous Brazilians and the Portuguese – spurned by both communities. São Paulo rose to become the centre of *bandeirante* activity in the 17th century and the *bandeirantes'* ignominious expeditions were responsible for the opening up of the country's interior and supplying the indigenous slave trade. A statue by one of Brazil's foremost modernist sculptors, Victor Brecheret, sits on the edge of Ibirapuera in homage to the *bandeirantes*. Yet whilst São Paulo was their headquarters, the *bandeirantes'* success in discovering gold led to the economic demise of the city in the 18th century. The inhabitants rushed to the gold fields in the *sertão*, leaving São Paulo to fall to ruin and fall under the influence of Rio de Janeiro. The relative backwardness of the region lasted until the late 19th century when the coffee trade spread west from Rio de Janeiro. Landowners became immensely rich. São Paulo changed from a small town into a financial and residential centre. Exports and imports flowed through Santos and the industrial powerhouse of the country was born. As the city boomed, industries and agriculture fanned outwards to the far reaches of the state.

Between 1885 and the end of the century the boom in coffee and the arrival of large numbers of Europeans transformed the state beyond recognition. By the end of the 1930s more than a million Italians, 500,000 Portuguese, nearly 400,000 Spaniards and 200,000 Japanese had arrived in São Paulo state. São Paulo now has the world's largest Japanese community outside Japan. Their main contribution to the economy has been in horticulture, raising poultry and cotton farming, especially around cities such as Marília. Nowadays, increasing numbers of Japanese-Brazilians work in the professions and the music industry. Significant numbers of Syrian-Lebanese arrived too, adding an extra dimension to the cultural diversity of the city. Many of the city's wealthiest dynasties are of Middle Eastern descent. São Paulo also has a large and successful Jewish community.

Much of the immigrant labour that flooded in during the early years of the 20th century was destined for the coffee *fazendas* and farms. Others went to work in the industries that were opening up in the city. By 1941 there were 14,000 factories and today the city covers more than 1500 sq km – three times the size of Paris – and greater São Paulo has a population of around 20 million.

Centro Histórico

São Paulo's city centre was once one of the most attractive in South America. English visitors in the 19th century described it as being spacious, green and dominated by terracotta-tiled buildings. There were even macaws and sloths in the trees. Today they are long gone and the centre is dominated by towering (and rather ugly) buildings, broken by a handful of interesting churches and cultural centres, and criss-crossed by narrow pedestrian streets. These are lined with stalls selling everything from shoes to electronics, second-hand goods and bric-a-brac, throughout the week. The best way to explore the area is by metrô and on foot, but don't stay after dark as the area is unsalubrious.

Praça da Sé and around → *Metrô Sé*.

The best place to begin a tour is at the **Praça da Sé**, an expansive square shaded by tropical trees and dominated by the hulking Catholic **Catedral Metropolitana** ① *Praça da Sé, T011-3107 6832, Mon-Sat 0800-1800, Sun 0830-1800, free, Metrô Sé*. This is the heart of the old city and has been the site of Brazil's largest public protests. Crowds gathered here in the late 1980s to demand the end to military rule. And, in 1992, they demanded the impeachment and resignation of the new Republic's second elected president, Fernando Collor – the first in a seemingly never-ending series of corrupt leaders who in 1990 had frozen the country's savings accounts and personally pocketed millions. The *praça* is always busy with hawkers, beggars, shoeshiners and business men rushing between meetings. Evangelists with megaphones proselytize on the steps of the cathedral – a symbol of the war between Christians for the souls of the poor that dominates contemporary urban Brazil. The *praça* is a great spot for street photography though be discreet with your camera and check that you aren't followed after taking your shots. Like São Paulo itself, the cathedral is more remarkable for its size than its beauty and is an unconvincing mish-mash of neo-Gothic and Renaissance. A narrow nave is squeezed uncomfortably between two monstrous 97-m-high spires beneath a bulbous copper cupola. It was designed in 1912 by the inappropriately named engineer Maximiliano Hell, inaugurated in the 1950s and fitted with its full complement of 14 towers only in 2002. The interior is bare but for a few stained glass windows designed in Germany and capitals decorated with Brazilian floral motifs. In the basement there is a vast, pseudo-Gothic crypt.

There are a few other sights of interest around the *praça*. Next door to the cathedral itself and housed in a 1930s art deco building is the **Conjunto Cultural da Caixa** ① *Praça*

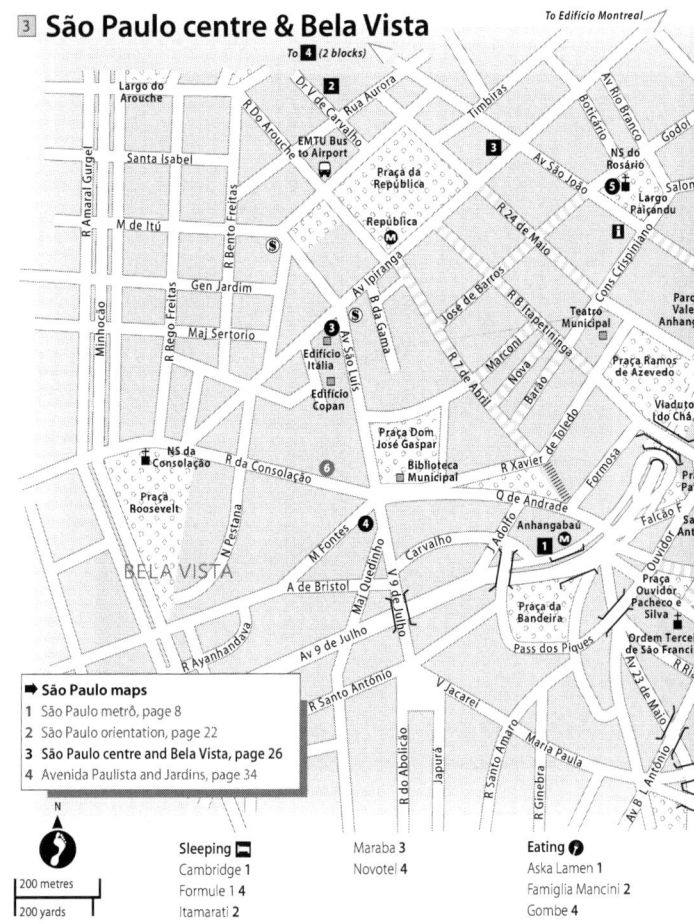

São Paulo centre & Bela Vista

➡ **São Paulo maps**
1 São Paulo metrô, page 8
2 São Paulo orientation, page 22
3 **São Paulo centre and Bela Vista, page 26**
4 Avenida Paulista and Jardíns, page 34

Sleeping
Cambridge 1
Formule 1 4
Itamarati 2
Maraba 3
Novotel 4

Eating
Aska Lamen 1
Famiglia Mancini 2
Gombe 4

26 • São Paulo Centro Histórico

da Sé 111, T011-3321 4400, www.caixacultural.com.br, Tue-Sun 0900-2100, US$2, Metrô Sé, a gallery that hosts excellent small international art and photography exhibitions by day, and, in the evenings, a boutique theatre. It also has a small banking museum with colonial furniture, on one of its upper floors. Two minutes' walk immediately to the west of the cathedral, squeezed between ugly modern buildings at the end of Rua Senador Feijó, is the **Igreja da Ordem Terceira de São Francisco** ① *Largo de São Francisco 133, T011-3106 0081, closed at time of publication, Metrô Sé*. This is one of the city's oldest churches, preserving a modest baroque interior (parts of which date to the 17th century) painted in celestial blue. It is quiet and meditative inside. The exterior is largely an 18th-century excrescence. The church is often referred to as 'O Convento de São Francisco' after a beautiful baroque convent that stood here until the 1930s. This was demolished along with vast swathes of the old colonial centre and sadly the Igreja da Ordem Terceira is in danger of undergoing the same fate – it was condemned in 2008 and remains closed pending donations for a restoration project. There are now only two churches in the centre of one of Brazil's oldest cities which retain any baroque remnants – the Igreja de Santo Antônio (see page 29) and the **Igreja da Ordem Terceira do Carmo** ① *R Rangel Pestana 230, Tue-Sun 0900-2100, free, Metrô Sé*. This church sits just off the far northeastern corner of the Praça da Sé, dates from 1632 and preserves its original gilt baroque altarpiece together with some other stucco work, religious paintings and artefacts. It is a peaceful little place in all the heat, hustle and bustle, and has with few visitors.

Pátio do Colégio and around → *Metrô Sé.*
The site of the founding of São Paulo can be reached by walking north from the bottom of the Praça da Sé (farthest from the cathedral) along Rua Santa Teresa and to the Praça Pátio do Colégio. Here lies the **Pátio do Colégio and Museu de Anchieta** ① *Praça Pátio do Colégio, T011-3105 6899, www.pateodocollegio.com.br, museum: Tue-Fri 0840-1630, US$3, free on the last Sun of the month, Metrô Sé*. Jesuit priests, led by 18-year-old Padre José de Anchieta arrived here in 1554, when the area was a tiny clearing on a hill in the midst of a vast

forest. They made camp and instructed their domicile indigenous Guarani to construct a simple wattle and daub hut. They inaugurated the building with a celebration of Mass on 25 January 1554, the feast of the conversion of São Paulo. Their simple hut took the saint's name, the 'Colégio de São Paulo de Piratinga'. The hut became a school for converted indigenous Brazilians seduced from the forests around. The school became a church and the church gave its name – São Paulo – to a settlement for *bandeirante* slaving raids into the Brazilian interior. In 1760, the Jesuits were expelled from the city they founded, for opposing the *bandeirantes* and their indigenous slave trade. But the Pátio do Colégio (as the complex of buildings came to be known) remained, becoming the palace of the fledgling province's Portuguese colonial captains general, and then of its Brazilian imperial governors. The church's tower fell down in 1886, and shortly after the whole building, but for one piece of wattle and daub wall, was demolished. The Jesuits didn't return to São Paulo until 1954 but they had long memories and immediately set about building an exact replica of their original church and college, which is what stands today. Most of the buildings are occupied by the **Museu Padre Anchieta**. This preserves, amongst other items, a modernist and not altogether sympathetic painting of the priest, by Italian Albino Menghini, bits of his corpse (which is now that of a saint after Anchieta was canonized by Pope John Paul II), a 17th-century font used to baptize the indigenous Brazilians and a collection of Guaraní art and artefacts from the colonial era. The Pátio has a great little al fresco café with a view, serving good snacks and light meals.

The exhibition spaces, cultural centres and concert halls of the **Centro Cultural Banco do Brasil** ⓘ *R Álvares Penteado 112, T011-3113 3651, www.bb.com.br, Mon-Fri 0900-1800, free except for exhibitions, Metrô Sé or São Bento*, can be reached by turning immediately west from the front of the Pátio do Colégio along Rua do Tesouro and then right for a block along Rua Álvares Penteado. These are housed in an attractive art deco building with a pretty glass ceiling. Many of the galleries are contained within the banks original vaults, some of which retain their massive iron doors. The cultural centre has a diverse programme of art and photography shows, cultural events and, in the evenings, theatre, music and cinema. It is always worth a visit in passing.

Mosteiro do São Bento and around → *Metrô São Bento.*

The most beautiful of all the churches in São Paulo is the Benedictine Basilica de Nossa Senhora de Assunção, known as the **Mosteiro São Bento** ⓘ *Largo São Bento, T011-3228 3633, www.mosteiro.org.br, Mon-Fri 0600-1800, Sat and Sun 0600-1200 and 1600-1800, Latin Mass with Gregorian chant Sun 1000; Latin vespers Mon-Fri 1725, Sat 1700, free, Metrô São Bento*. Benedictines arrived on this site in 1598, shortly after the Jesuits and, like them, proceeded to proselytize the indigenous people. Despite their long history in the city the monastery is a modern church dating from 1914. It was designed by Munich-based architect Richard Bernl in homage to the English Norman style. Its façade is strikingly similar to Southwell cathedral in Nottinghamshire, though with added Rhineland roofs and baroque revival flourishes. But few visit São Bento for the exterior. The church preserves a striking Beuronese interior painted by Dom Adelbert Gresnicht, a Dutch Benedictine monk. The style is named after techniques developed by Benedictines in the monastery of Beuron in southwest Germany in the late 19th and early 20th centuries. It finds much inspiration in Byzantine art and is characterized by compressed perspective and iconic, almost exaggerated colours. São Bento is one of the finest Beuronese churches in the world. The stained glass (and much of the statuary) is also by Dom Adelbert. Most of the windows show scenes from the life of St Benedict with the most beautiful, at the far end of the nave, showing Our Lady ascending to heaven guided by the Holy Spirit in the form of a dove. The church has Brazil's finest organ which is given its own festival in November and December every year. And with this being a Benedictine monastery, there is of course a temple to commerce: the shop sells delicious sweets home-made by the monks in their bakery.

Immediately in front of the monastery, at the corner of Avenida São João and Rua Libero Badaró, is the **Edifício Martinelli (Martinelli Building)** ① *Av São João 35, not open to the public, Metrô São Bento*. This was the city's first skyscraper and, when it was built, looked out over a sea of terracotta roofs and handsome tree-lined avenues. The building is reminiscent of New York's upper east side but is by no means as distinguished: while colonial São Paulo was unique and beautiful, the buildings that replaced it looked tawdry and crowded next to the New York it longed to imitate.

Around the corner is another architectural pastiche, the **Edifício Altino Arantes** (aka **Edifício Banespa/Santander Cultural**) ① *R João Bricola 24 (Metrô São Bento), T011-3249 7466, Mon-Fri 1000-1500, free, passport ID is required, visits limited to 10 mins (dusk visits are limited to those with prior appointments), daypacks must be left in reception, no tripods or bags can be taken to the viewing deck*, looking a bit like a wan Empire State Building, small enough to collapse under the weight of King Kong. The view of the city from the observatory is awe-inspiring. On its fringes are the vast favelas and new distant neighbourhoods with infant skyscraper flats and hundreds of helicopters whirling busily overhead like giant buzzing flies.

Less than 50 m from the Edifício Altino Arantes is the oldest church in São Paulo's city centre, the **Igreja de Santo Antônio** ① *Praça do Patriarca s/n, Mon-Fri 0900-1600, free, Metrô São Bento*, with parts dating from 1592. It was fully restored in 2005 and together with the Igreja do Carmo is the only church in the city centre with a baroque interior – although much of what you see today is from reforms in 1899. It's a tranquil spot in the middle of one of the world's busiest city centres.

The streets between São Bento and Luz are some of the busiest shopping districts in the city. The partially covered **Rua 25 de Março** ① *daily 0700-1800, Metrô São Bento shopping complex*, runs north to Rua Paula Sousa and Luz Metrô station. Two blocks to the east of 25 de Marco along Rua Comendador Afonso Kherlakian is the beautiful art deco **Mercado Municipal** ① *R da Cantareira 306, Centro, T011-3326 3401, www.mercado municipal.com.br, Mon-Sat 0600-1800, Sun 0600-1600, free, Metrô São Bento or Luz* (see page 59). The area offers some of the best people-watching and shopping adventures in the city. It's an easy walk from the market or Rua 25 de Março to Luz, though caution should be observed at all times. The streets to the west, between the centre and Júlio Prestes station, should be avoided. This is a notorious area for crack dealing.

Praça da República → *Metrô República.*

There are a few interesting sites here. Most notable is the **Edifício and Terraço Itália** ① *Av Ipiranga 344, T011-2189 2990 and T011-2189 2929, www.edificioitalia.com.br, restaurant: www.terracoitalia.com.br, US$8, Metrô República*, a rather unremarkable restaurant in the city's tallest building with a truly remarkable view from the observation deck. Arrive half an hour before sunset for the best balance of natural and artificial light, and bring a tripod.

The skyscraper immediately in front of the *terraço* is Oscar Niemeyer's **Edifício Copan** ① *Av Ipiranga 200, not open to the public though some visitors are allowed to go to the terraço at the discretion of security*, Metrô República, built in 1951 in a spate of design by the architect, which also included the nearby **Edifício Montreal** ① *Av Ipiranga at Cásper Líbero*, and the **Edifício Califórnia** ① *R Barão de Itapetininga*. Edifício Copan was the setting for a series of memorable short stories, dissecting daily life and class in São Paulo written by the Paulistano writer Regina Rheda, and published in English as *First World, Third Class and Other Tales of the Global Mix* in 2005.

From the corner of Praça da República, a 10-minute walk southeast along Rua 24 de Maio brings you back into the main part of the city centre and Metrô Anhangabaú, via the **Teatro Municipal Opera House** ① *Praça Ramos de Azevedo s/n, T011-3397 0300, www.prefeitura.sp.gov.br/cidade/secretarias/cultura/teatromunicipal/, box office Mon-Fri 1000-1900, Sat 1000-1700, tickets from US$5, Metrô Anhangabaú, República or São Bento*, based on the 1874 Beaux-Arts, Palais Garnier, but stunted in comparison, in dull stone and with huge baroque flourishes on the roof which make it look rather ridiculous. Maria Callas, Nureyev and Fonteyn and Duke Ellington have all graced the concert hall and the venue continues to host a slice of the better classical music, theatre and ballet performances in the city. Next to the theatre is the **Viaduto do Chá**, a steel bridge riding over the attractive but scruffy Vale de Anhangabaú park and the traffic-heavy Avenida 23 de Maio and 9 de Julho urban highways.

North of the centre

Luz → *Metrô Luz or Metrô Tiradentes, CPTM Luz or Júlio Prestes.*

Some of São Paulo's finest museums are to be found a few kilometres north of the city centre in the neighbourhood of Luz. The area is dominated by two striking 19th- and early 20th-century railway stations, both in use today: the **Estação da Luz** ① *Praça da Luz 1, T0800-550121 for information on suburban trains*, and **Estação Júlio Prestes** ① *Praça Júlio Prestes 51, www.estacoesferroviarias.com.br/j/jprestes.htm*. The former marked the realization of a dream for O Ireneu Evangelista de Sousa, the Visconde de Mauá, who was Brazil's first industrial magnate. A visit to London in the 1840s convinced de Sousa that Brazil's future lay in rapid industrialization – a path he followed with the founding of an ironworks employing some 300 workers from England and Scotland. It made him a millionaire and in 1854 he opened his first railway, designed and run by the British. It linked Jundiaí, in the heart of the São Paulo coffee region, with Santos on the coast via what was then the relatively small city of São Paulo. The line is still extant; though passenger trains only run on the Jundiaí to São Paulo section (see Linha 7 Rubi, page 62). The grandness of the Estação de Luz station, which was completed in 1900, attests to the fact that the city quickly grew wealthy by exploiting its position at the railway junction. By the time the Estação Júlio Prestes was built, Britannia no longer ruled the railways. This next station was modelled on Grand Central and Penn in New York. In 1999 the enormous 1000-sq-m grand hall was converted into the magnificent, cathedral-like **Sala São Paulo concert hall** ① *Praça Júlio Prestes 51, T011-3337 9573, www.salasaopaulo.art.br, guided visits Mon-Fri 1300-1630, Sat 1330, Sun 1400 (when there is an evening performance) or 1230 (when there is an afternoon performance), US$2.50, free on weekends, foreigners should book ahead through the website as English-speaking guides must be arranged, box office*

T011-3223 3966, Mon-Fri 1000-1800, Sat 1000-1630, concerts from US$10, Metrô Luz, CPTM Luz or Júlio Prestes, Brazil's most prestigious classical music venue (see page 56).

The city's finest collection of Brazilian art lies 100 m from the Estação da Luz in the **Pinacoteca do Estado** ① *Praça da Luz 2, T011-3324 0933, www.pinacoteca.org.br, Tue-Sun 1000-1800 (last entry at 1730), Sat 1000-1730, US$3, free on Sat, Metrô Luz, CPTM Luz, excellent museum shop and café.* Here you will find works by Brazilian artists from the colonial and imperial eras, together with paintings by the founders of Brazilian modernism, such as Lasar Segall, Tarsila do Amaral, Candido Portinari and Alfredo Volpi. The gallery also contains sculpture by Rodin, Victor Brecheret and contemporary works by artists such as the Nipo-Brazilian painter Tomie Ohtake. The excellent photography gallery in the basement displays some of the world's greatest black-and-white photographers, many of whom are from Brazil. The museum overlooks the **Parque da Luz**, a lovely shady green space dotted with modernist sculpture and shaded by large tropical figs and palms. Take care in this area after dark.

The Pinacoteca's sister gallery, the **Estação Pinacoteca and Memorial da Resistência museum** ① *Largo General Osório 66, T011-3337 0185, daily 1000-1730, US$2, free for the Memorial da Resistência a*nd for the galleries on Sat, very good café restaurant, Metrô Luz, CPTM Luz and Júlio Prestes, is just over 500 m west of the Pinacoteca along Rua Mauá, next to the Estação Júlio Prestes and Sala São Paulo. It houses 200 of the country's finest modernist paintings from the archive of fthe Fundação José e Paulina Nemirovsky, including further key pieces by Tarsila do Amaral, Emiliano Di Cavalcanti, Portinari Anita Malfatti, Victor Brecheret and Lasar Segall. International art includes Chagall, Picasso and Braque. The building was once the headquarters of the Departamento Estadual de Ordem Politica e Social do Estado de São Paulo (DEOPS/SP) – the counter-insurgency wing of the Policia Militar police force. Thousands of Paulistanos were tortured and killed here between 1940 and 1983, during the Vargas years and the military dictatorship. The Memorial da Resistência de São Paulo museum on the ground floor tells their story in grisly detail – through panels, documents and photographs – and shows how the CIA supported the oppression.

Luz's other excellent museum is the **Museu de Arte Sacra** ① *Av Tiradentes 676, 400 m north of the Pinacoteca, T011-3227 7687, www.museuartesacra.org.br, Mon-Fri 1000-1700, Sat and Sun 1000-1900, US$2, Metrô Tiradentes, CPTM Luz.* This superb little museum is often overlooked by visitors, yet it is one of the finest of its kind in the Americas and lies almost immediately opposite the Pinacoteca. The collection is housed in a large wing of one of the city's most distinguished colonial buildings, the early 19th-century Mosteiro da Luz. Parts of the monastery are still home to Conceptionist sisters and the entire complex is imbued with a restful sense of serenity. Even those who are not interested in church art will find the galleries a delightfully peaceful haven from the frenetic chaos of São Paulo. The collection, however, is priceless and of international importance. Rooms house various objects and artefacts – from lavish monstrances and ecclesiastical jewellery to church altarpieces. Of particular note is the statuary, with pieces by many of the most important Brazilian baroque masters. Amongst objects by Aleijadinho, Mestre Valentim and Frei Agostinho da Piedade is a wonderful Mary Magdalene by Francisco Xavier de Brito, displaying an effortless unity of motion and melancholy contemplation. There are sculptures by (anonymous) Brazilian indigenous artists, a majestic African-Brazilian São Bento (with blue eyes) and an extraordinarily detailed 18th-century Neapolitan nativity crib comprising almost 2000 pieces, which is the most important of its kind outside Naples.

Barra Funda and Higienópolis → *Metrô Palmeiras-Barra Funda, CPTM Barra Funda.*

The monumentalist group of modernist concrete buildings making up the **Memorial da América Latina** ⓘ *Av Mário de Andrade 664, next to Metrô Barra Funda, T011-3823 4600, www.memorial.org.br, Tue-Fri 0900-2100, Sat 0900-1800, Sun 1000-1800, free,* were designed by **Oscar Niemeyer** and built in March 1989. They comprise a monumental 85000-sq-m-complex of curvi-linear galleries, conference spaces, walkways, bridges and squares, broken by an ugly, urban highway and dotted with imposing sculptures. The largest of these is in the shape of an outstretched hand. The complex was built with the grand aim of integrating Latin American nations, culturally and politically, but it is sorely underused. Occasional shows (details on the website) include the annual Latin American art exhibition in the Pavilhão de Criatividade.

A few kilometres west of Barra Funda – and a quick hop along the CPTM's Linha Rubi, in the emerging nightlife district of **Água Branca**, is **SESC Pompeia** ⓘ *R Clélia 93, T011-3871 7700, www.sescsp.org.br, CPTM Água Branca, 10 minswalk southeast or US$3 in a taxi,* an arts complex housed in a striking post-industrial building designed by Lina Bo Bardi (see page 53), which together with SESC Vila Mariana (see page 37) showcases some of the best medium-sized musical acts in the city – names like João Bosco, CéU and Otto. It is a vibrant place, with a theatre, exhibitions, workshops, restaurant and café, as well as a gym and areas for sunbathing and watching television.

The upper middle-class neighbourhood of **Higienópolis** lies between Barra Funda and Consolação. It is a favourite haunt of artists and musicians; particularly the **Bretagne building** ⓘ *Av Higienópolis 938, T011-3667 2516,* one of a handful of delightful mid-20th-century blocks of flats whose curved lines, brilliant mosaics and polished stone looks like a film set for an arty 1960s picture. Higienópolis also boasts one of the city's plushest shopping malls, the **Patio Higienópolis** ⓘ *Av Higienópolis 618, T011-3823 2300, www.patiohigienopolis.com.br.*

West of the centre

Avenida Paulista → *Metrô Vergueiro or Paraíso for the southeastern end of Paulista.*

Southwest of the Centro Histórico, Avenida Paulista, is lined by skyscrapers and is thick with six lanes of cars. It is one of São Paulo's classic postcard shots and locals like to compare it to Fifth Avenue in New York. In truth, it's more commercial and lined with functional buildings, most of which are unremarkable individually and awe-inspiring as a whole.

The avenue was founded in 1891 by the Uruguayan engineer Joaquim Eugênio de Lima, who wanted to build a Paulistano Champs-Élysées. After he built a mansion on Avenida Paulista, many coffee barons followed suit and by the early 20th century, Paulista had become the city's most fashionable promenade. The mansions and the rows of stately trees that sat in front of them were almost all demolished in the 1940s and 1950s to make way for ugly office buildings, and in the 1980s these were in turn demolished as banks and multinationals established their headquarters here.

The highlight of Avenida Paulista is the **Museu de Arte de São Paulo (MASP)** ⓘ *Av Paulista 1578, T011-3251 5644, www.masp.art.br, Tue-Wed and Fri-Sun 1100-1800, Thu 1100-1900, US$5, Metrô Trianon-MASP.* This is the most important gallery in the southern hemisphere, preserving some of Europe's greatest paintings. If it were in the US or Europe it would be as busy as the Prado or the Guggenheim, but here, aside from the occasional noisy group of schoolchildren, the gallery is invariably deserted. Even at weekends, visitors can stop and stare at a Rembrandt or a Velazquez at their leisure. The museum has a far larger collection than it is able to display and only a tiny fraction reaches the walls of the modest-sized international gallery. France gets star-billing, with 11 Renoirs, 70 Degas, and a stream of works by Monet, Manet, Cezanne, Toulouse-Lautrec and Gauguin. Renaissance Italy is represented by a Raphael Resurrection, an impeccable Bellini and a series of exquisite late 15th-century icons. The remaining walls are adorned with paintings by Bosch, Goya, Van Dyck, Turner, Constable and many others, cherry-picked from post-War Europe. A gallery downstairs, the Galeria Clemente de Faria, houses temporary exhibitions, mostly by contemporary Brazilian artists and photographers, and the museum has a decent and good-value restaurant serving buffet lunches (see page 48) and a small gift shop. On Sunday, an antiques fair is held in the open space beneath the museum.

Opposite MASP is the **Parque Tenente Siqueira Campos** ⓘ *R Peixoto Gomide 949 and Av Paulista, daily 0700-1830*, also known as Parque Trianon, covering two blocks on either side of Alameda Santos. It is a welcome, luxuriant, green area located in what is now the busiest part of the city. The vegetation includes native plants typical of the *Mata Atlântica*. Next to the park is the smaller Praça Alexandre de Gusmão.

Consolação and the Pacaembu Museu do Futebol → *Metrô Consolação.*

Consolação, which lies between the northeastern end of Avenida Paulista and the Edifício Italia and Praça República in the city centre, is emerging as the edgiest and most exciting nocturnal neighbourhood in São Paulo. Until a few years it was home to little more than rats, sleazy strip bars, street-walkers and curb-crawlers, but now it harbours a thriving alternative weekend scene. Its untidy streets are lined with grafitti-scrawled shop fronts, the deep velvet-red of open bar doors, go-go clubs with heavy-set bouncers outside and makeshift street bars. On Fridays and Saturdays from 2200 a jostle of hundreds of young Paulistanos down bottles of cooler-fresh Bohemia beer at rickety metal tables, and lines of sharply dressed and well-toned 20- and 30-somethings queue to enter a gamut of fashionable bars, clubs and pounding gay venues, including one of Brazil's most exciting underground venues: **Studio SP** (see Bars and clubs, page 53).

Just north of Consolação, on the other side of the Sacramento Cemetery and rushing Avenida Doutour Arnaldo, is the beautiful art deco **Estádio Pacaembu** which hosts domestic games and big international rock concerts. It sits in a square named after Charles Miller, the Englishman who brought football to Brazil. Inside is the **Museu do Futebol** ⓘ *Metrô Clinicas, Estádio do Pacaembu, Praça Charles Miller, T011-3663 3848, www.museudofutebol.org.br, Tue-Sun 1000-1700, US$3, free on Thu, children under 7 go free, restaurants next to the museum in the stadium, Metrô Sumaré (20-min walk)*, which cost US$15 million and which was inaugurated by Pelé in September 2008. The World Cup, which Brazil have won more often than any other team, is the principal focus. One gallery is devoted to the tournament, profiling the games and what was happening in the world at the time, and telling both stories through video footage, photographs, memorabilia and newspaper cuttings. Music from the likes of Ary Barroso and Jorge Ben forms the soundtrack, along with recordings of cheering fans. A second gallery showcases Brazil's greatest stars, including Garrincha, Falcão, Zico, Bebeto, Didi, Romário, Ronaldo, Gilmar, Gérson, Sócrates, Rivelino, Ronaldo (who is known as Ronaldinho or Ronaldinho

Fenomeno in Brazil) and, of course, Pelé. The shirt he wore during the 1970 World Cup final – a game frequently cited as the greatest ever played when Brazil beat Italy 4-1 to take the title for the third time – receives pride of place. A third gallery is more interactive, offering visitors the chance to dribble and shoot at goals and test their knowledge on football facts and figures.

Jardins → *Metrô Consolação or Oscar Freire (Linha Amarela from 2012).*

Immediately west of Avenida Paulista, an easy 10-minute walk from Consolação Metrô along Rua Haddock Lobo, is the plush neighbourhood of Jardins. This is by far the most pleasant area to stay in São Paulo; it has the best restaurants, shops and cafés and is a tranquil spot for a strong coffee and people-watching, or an urban boutique browse. Jardins is in reality a series of neighbourhoods – each with its own name – the stretches closest to Paulista are known as **Cerqueira César** (to the northwest) and **Jardim Paulista** (to the southeast). These two areas have the bulk of the boutique shops, swanky hotels and chic restaurants. The most self-consciously chic of all is the cross section between Rua

Avenida Paulista & Jardins

➡ **São Paulo maps**
1 São Paulo metrô, page 8
2 São Paulo orientation, page 22
3 São Paulo centre and Bela Vista, page 26
4 Avenida Paulista and Jardins, page 34

Oscar Freire, Rua Bela Cintra and Rua Haddock Lobo, where even the poodles wear collars with designer labels and everyone, from the shop owner to the doorman, addresses people as '*Querida*' (Darling).

Immediately west of Jardim Paulista and Cerqueira César, and separated from those neighbourhoods by a stately city highway preserving a handful of coffee Baron mansions (Avenida Brasil), are three more Jardins. **Jardim Paulistano** is dominated by Avenida Gabriel Monteiro da Silva, which is lined by very expensive, internationally reknowned home decor and furniture stores. Between Jardim Paulistano and Ibirapuera Park are **Jardim America** and **Jardim Europa**, both made up of leafy streets lined with vast mansion houses, almost completely hidden behind towering walls topped with razor wire and formidable electric fencing. Their idyllic seclusion is spoilt only by the stench of raw favela sewage from the nearby River Pinheiros.

The **Museu Brasileiro da Escultura** (**MUBE**) ① *Av Europa 218, T011-2594 2601, www.mube.art.br, Tue-Sun 1000-1900, free,* showcases contemporary Brazilian sculpture through visiting exhibitions. Most are rather lacklustre and the museum merits a visit more for the building itself, which is by Brazil's Prtizker prize-winning architect Paulo Mendes da Rocha. Like many Brazilian architects Espírito Santo-born Rocha is celebrated for his inventive, minimalist use of concrete. The museum is made up of a series of massive, grey, bunker-like concrete blocks which contrast starkly with the surrounding gardens (by Burle Marx), but which integrate them with the underground exhibition spaces. To get there from Metrô Consolação, take bus 702P-42, marked 'Butantã', from the corner of Rua Augusta and Avenida Paulista.

The **Museu da Casa Brasileira** ① *Av Brigadeiro Faria Lima 2705, T011-3032 3727, Tue-Sun 1000-1800, US$2,* preserves a collection of antique (mostly baroque) Brazilian and Portuguese and contemporary international furniture in one of the few remaining coffee baron mansions. The museum also hosts the annual Prêmio Design MCB design awards, which has become one of the most celebrated in Brazil. Temporary exhibition spaces showcase the winners and the museum has a pleasant garden (with live music on Sundays) and a good café-restaurant. From CPTM Cidade Jardim it's 10 minutes' walk; from Pinheiros head east along Rua Professor Artur Ramos to Avenida Brigadeiro Faria Lima.

Transamérica Ópera **13** *B2*
Unique & Skye Bar **14** *C2*

Eating
America **3** *B3*
A Mineira **1** *C3*
Baalbeck **2** *B2*
Chariô Bistro **5** *B2*
Cheiro Verde **6** *B2*
Dalva e Dito **4** *B2*
DOM **7** *B2*
Dui **8** *A2*
Figueira Rubaiyat **16** *B1*
Frans Café **12** *C3*
Gero **9** *B1*
Jun Sakamoto **10** *A1*
Kayomix **11** *B2*
La Tambouille **24** *C1*
Mani **25** *B1*
Marakuthai **15** *B3*
MASP **13** *B3*
Massimo **14** *B2*
Sattva **17** *B2*
Spot **19** *B3*
Sujinho **18** *A3*

Bars & clubs
Balcão **21** *A2*
Casa de Franciscka **20** *C3*
Dry Bar **26** *B2*
Finnegan's Pub **22** *A1*
Mokai **27** *B2*
Outs Club **23** *A3*
Sonique Club **28** *A3*
Studio SP **29** *B3*
Vegas Club **31** *A3*
Volt **32** *A3*

Vila Madalena and Pinheiros → *Metrô Madalena.*

If Jardins is São Paulo's upper East Side or Bond Street, Vila Madalena and neighbouring Pinheiros are its East Village or Notting Hill – still fashionable, but younger, less ostentatiously moneyed and with more of a skip in their step. Streets are crammed with bars, restaurants and an array of the city's freshest designer labels, clambering over the steep hills and buzzing with young and arty middle-class Paulistanos. Younger boutique brands have set up shop in Vila Madalena (see Shopping, page 57). Galleries such as **Choque Cultural** ① *R João Moura 197, T011-3061 4051, Mon-Fri 1000-1700, Sat 1100-1700, www.choquecultural.co.uk*, sell work by the newest wave of the city's increasingly famous street artists (as well as prints available online through their UK website).

There's music on every corner in both neighbourhoods – from spit-and-sawdust samba bars to mock-Bahian *forró* clubs and well-established live music venues. The area attracts the artistically rich and famous: Seu Jorge lives and drinks in Vila Madalena, as does leading avant garde musician, Max de Castro. The only sight of any consequence is the **Instituto Tomie Ohtake** ① *R dos Coropés 88, T011-3814 0705, www.instituto tomieohtake.org.br, Tue-Fri 1000-1800, US$3*, a monolithic, rather ungainly red and purple tower by Unique Hotel architect Ruy Ohtake. It has galleries inside devoted to the work of his Japanese-Brazilian artist mother, Tomie, and a series of other exhibition halls with work by up-and-coming artists. To get there, go to Metrô Vila Madalena, then take bus 701-10 southwest along Rua Purpurina and Rua Fradique Coutinho, getting off at the stop at Fradique Coutinho 1331. Leave the stop and turn right onto Rua Wisard. After 200 m continue onto Rua dos Miranhas. After 400 m continue onto Rua dos Tamanás and after 150 m turn right into Rua dos Coropés.

South of the centre

Liberdade → *Metrô Liberdade.*

Liberdade was the first centre for the Japanese community in São Paulo; a city with more ethnic Japanese than any other outside Japan. It lies directly south of the Praça da Sé and can easily be reached on foot in under 10 minutes. There are all manner of Asian shops selling everything from woks to *manga* and the streets are illuminated by lights designed to resemble Japanese lanterns. A market selling Asian produce and food is held every Sunday in the Praça da Liberdade and there are many excellent Japanese restaurants.

The **Museu da Imigração Japonesa** ① *R São Joaquim 381, 3rd floor, T011-3209 5465, www.nihonsite.com/muse, Tue-Sun 1330-1730, US$3, Metrô Liberdade*, in the Japanese-Brazilian cultural centre, is a modern, well-kept little museum with exhibitions telling the story of the Japanese migration to Brazil, a replica of the first ship that brought the Japanese to Brazil, reconstructions of early Japanese Brazilian houses, artefacts.

Bela Vista

Bela Vista lies immediately west of Liberdade and east of Consolação between the city centre and Avenida Paulista. In the late 19th and early 20th century the neighbourhood was a centre of Italian immigration. It is a higgledy-piggledy mass of small streets lined with residential houses. There are few sights of interest but the area is a pleasant place for a wander – especially at weekends. On Sunday there is an antiques market, the **Feira das Antiguidades** ① *Praça Dom Orione, Bixiga, Bela Vista, Sun 1000-1500*, sometimes with live *chorinho*. There are Italianate houses nearby on Rua dos Ingleses, and a number of little cafés and bars. During carnival the **Vai Vai samba school** ⓘ *R São Vicente 276, T011-3266 2581, www.vaivai.com.br, US$6 for the carnival party*, opens its doors to as many as 4000 visitors who come to dance samba and process through the nearby streets. They often throw a smaller *feijoada* party at weekends. **Rua Avanhandava**, which runs off Rua Martins Fontes in the north of Bela Vista, was closed to traffic in 2007, and has since become one of the prettiest streets in the neighbourhood, lined with some traditional Italian restaurants.

Paraíso and Vila Mariana

Southwest of Liberdade and beginning where Avenida Paulista becomes Rua Vergueiro, are the neighbourhoods of Paraíso and Vila Mariana. Paraíso is dominated by the hulking dome of the the **Catedral Ortodoxa** ⓘ *R Vergueiro 1515, Paraíso, T011-5579 3835, www.catedralortodoxa.com.br, Mon-Fri 0900-1300 and 1500-1800, Sat 1000-1300, Mass at 1015 on Sun, Metrô Paraíso*. The church is modelled on the Hagia Sofia in Istanbul and is one of the largest Antiochian Orthodox churches in the world. Most of the worshippers are Brazilians of Syrian and Lebanese descent. The church of Antioch is one of the five original churches and was founded in Antioch, Turkey by the apostles Peter and Paul. It's seat is in Damascus, Syria and the current patriarch is His Beatitude Patriarch Ignatius IV (Hazim) of Antioch and all the East. Vila Mariana is principally a residential neighbourhood abutting Ibirapuera park. The **SESC Vila Mariana** ⓘ *R Pelotas 141, Vila Mariana, T011-5080 3000, www.sescsp.org.br, daily 1000-2000*, is a cultural centre with a swimming pool, internet, a gym and a concert hall which hosts some of the best small acts in São Paulo. From Metrô Ana Rosa, it's 10 minutes' walk south of Ana Rosa, east along Avenida Cnso Rodrigues Alves, right onto Rua Humberto I (after 500 m) and left onto Pelotas (after 200 m).

Parque do Ibirapuera

ⓘ *Entrance on Av Pedro Álvares Cabral, daily 0500-2400, T011-5573 4180, www.parquedo ibirapuera.com, free, unsafe after dark, www.parquedoibirapuera.com. Metrô Ana Rosa is a 15-min walk east of the park: turn right out of the station and walk due west along Av Conselheiro Rodrigo Alves, continue onto Av Dante Pazzanese which comes to the Av 23 de Maio urban freeway, the park sits in front of you on the other side of the road and can be reached via a footbridge 200 m to the right in front of the Detran building; alternatively bus 5164-21 (marked Cidade Leonor, direção Parque do Ibirapuera) leaves every 30 mins from Metrô Santa Cruz for Ibirapuera; any bus to DETRAN (the Driver and Vehicle licensing building, labelled in huge letters) stops opposite Ibirapuera. Lines include 175T-10, 477U-10 and 675N-10.*

The park was designed by architect Oscar Niemeyer and landscape artist Roberto Burle Marx for the city's fourth centenary in 1954. It is the largest of the very few green spaces in central São Paulo and its shady woodlands, lawns and lakes offer a breath of fresher air in a city that has only 4.6 sq m of vegetation per inhabitant. The park is also home to a number of museums and monuments and some striking Oscar Niemeyer buildings that were designed in the 1950s but which have only been constructed in the last five years. These include the Pavilhão Lucas Nogueira Garcez, most commonly referred to as the **Oca** ⓘ *Portão 3, open for exhibitions*, a brilliant white, polished concrete dome, built in homage to an indigenous Brazilian roundhouse. It stages major international art exhibitions (see the Ibirapuera website, above, for what's on). Next to it is the **Auditório**

Ibirapuera ① *Portão 3, www.auditorioibirapuera.com.br*, a concert hall shaped like a giant wedge. The **Fundação Bienal** ① *Portão 3, http://bienalsaopaulo.globo.com, open for exhibitions*, (Bienal buildings) are also by Niemeyer and house the city's flagship fashion and art events: the twice yearly São Paulo fashion week and the **Art Biennial**, the most important events of their kind in the southern hemisphere.

A **sculpture garden** separates the Bienal from the Oca; this garden is watched over by the **Museu de Arte Moderna** (**MAM**) ① *Portão 3, T011-5085 1300, www.mam.org.br, Tue-Sun 1000-1800 (ticket office closes at 1730), US$2.50*. This small museum, with a giant mural outside by Os Gêmeos, showcases the best Brazilian contemporary art in temporary exhibitions. There is always something worth seeing and the gallery has an excellent buffet restaurant and gift shop. MAM is linked by a covered walkway to the **Museu Afro-Brasil** ① *Portão 10, T011-4004 5006, www.museuafro brasil.com.br, Tue-Sun 1000-1800, US$4*, which lies inside Niemeyer's spectacular, stilted **Pavilhão Manoel da Nobrega** building and devotes more than 12,000 sq m to a celebration of black Brazilian culture with regular films, music, dance, and theatrical events and an archive of over 5000 photographs, paintings, ritual objects and artefacts which include the bisected hull of a slaving ship showing the conditions under which Africans were brought to Brazil.

A few hundred metres to the west of here, on the shores of the artificial lake, the **Planetário e Museu de Astronomia Professor Aristóteles Orsini** (**Planetarium**) ① *Portão 10, T011-5575 5206, www.prefeitura.sp.gov.br/astronomia, Sat and Sun 1200- 1800, US$5*, was restored in 2006 with a new projection ceiling and state-of-the-art Star Master projection equipment by Carl Zeiss, and is now one of the most impressive in Latin America. Shows are in Portuguese.

Less than 100 m to the south, is the **Pavilhão Japonês** ① *Portão 10, T011-5081 7296, Wed, Sat, Sun and holidays 1300-1700, free except for exhibitions*. The building is a reproduction of the Palácio Katsura, in Tokyo, built in Japan in strict adherence to Japanese aesthetic principles and re-assembled next to the park's largest lake (which has illuminated fountain displays on weekday evenings). The pavilion on the lower floor has an exhibition space devoted to Japanese-Brazilian and Japanese culture and a traditional Japanese tearoom upstairs.

The park also has a **running track** (with pit stops for exercise with pull-up bars, weight machines and chunky wooden dumbells), football pitches and hosts regular open-air concerts on Sundays. Those seeking something quieter on a Sunday can borrow a book from the portable library and read it in the shade of the **Bosque da Leitura** or 'reading wood'. Bicycles can be hired in the park (US$3 per hour) and there are dozens of small snack vendors and café-restaurants.

Ibirapuera also has a few monuments of note. **O Monumento as Bandeiras**, which sits on the northern edge of the park, is a brutalist tribute to the marauding and bloodthirsty slave traders, or *bandeirantes*, who opened up the interior of Brazil. It was created by Brazil's foremost 20th-century sculptor, Victor Brecheret. The **Obelisco aos Héroes de 32**, on the eastern edge of the park, is a monumental Cleopatra's needle built in honour of the Paulistano rebels who died in 1932 when the dictator Getúlio Vargas crushed resistance to his Estado Novo regime. Above the rushing Sena Madureira urban highway – where it thunders into the tunnel which passes beneath the park – is **Velocidade, Alma e Emoção** (Speed, Soul and Emotion), a bronze tribute to one of São Paulo's favourite sons, the Formula One driver **Ayrton Senna**, by local artist Melinda Garcia.

A bridge leads across the 16-lane Avenida 23 de Maio urban highway in the southeast corner of the park near Portao 4 to the former DETRAN building, which is a giant oblong on stilts by Oscar Niemeyer. Until 2007 it was home to the state transit authority. In late 2011 it is ostensibly due to reopen as the new home of the **Museu de Arte Contemporanea de São Paulo (MAC)**.

Itaim Bibi, Vila Olímpia and Moema → *Metrô Faria Lima (from 2012), CPTM Vila Olímpia and Cidade Jardim.*

Business mixes with pleasure in these plush neighbourhoods south of Jardins and near Ibirapuera park. By day they are filled with office workers; by night, especially at weekends, hundreds of street bars and clubs are busy with partying Paulistano professionals. There are also many glamorous shops, including the city's notorious temple to excess, **Daslu**, see page 60, a shop so exclusive that it sits behind its own security gate, shirks changing rooms in favour of women- and men-only shopping galleries, and which boasts a roof covered in helipads for its preferred clientele. It is possible to spend a fortune and an entire day in Daslu, which is dotted with exclusive cafés and restaurants and even has its own private party area on the upper floor.

Further afield

Brooklin and the New Business District → *Metrô Brooklin.*

Brooklin's Avenida Engenheiro Luís Carlos Berrini has taken over from Avenida Paulista as the business centre of the new São Paulo. Many of the larger companies, banks and international corporations now have their South American headquarters here, making this a likely centre of operations for those visiting the city for a work trip.

Parque do Estado

This large park housing the botanical and zoological gardens is 15 km south of the centre at **Água Funda**. The **Jardim Botânico** ⓘ *Av Miguel Estefano s/n, Agua Funda, T011-5073 6300, www.ibot.sp.gov.br, Tue-Sun 0900-1700, US$1.50, Metrô São Judas and then bus 4742 marked Jardim Climax, or taxi from Metrô Jabaquara (US$8)*, has a vast garden esplanade surrounded by magnificent stone porches, with lakes and trees and places for picnics, and a very fine orchid farm worth seeing during the flowering season (November to December). More than 19,000 different kinds of orchids are cultivated. There are orchid exhibitions in April and November. The astronomical **observatory** nearby is open to the public on Thursday afternoons. Howler monkeys, guans and toco toucans can be seen near the end of the day. To get there take the metrô to São Judas on the Jabaquara line, then take a bus.

The **Jardim Zoológico** ⓘ *Av Miguel Estefano 4241, Água Funda, T011-5073 0811, www.zoologico.com.br, Tue-Sun 0900-1700, US$7, children 7-12 US$3, children under 7 free, Metrô Jabaquara (shuttle from the metrô station to the zoo, US$2, tickets to the zoo can be bought at the metrô ticket office in Jabaquara)*, is the biggest zoo in the country and claims that it is the fourth biggest in the world, with 3200 animals, including the big international mammals and many rare and endangered Brazilian species. These include jaguar, puma (in small enclosures), Spix's macaw (which is extinct in the wild), Lear's macaw (which is critically endangered), Harpy eagle, bush dog and maned wolf.

Butantã and the Cidade Universitária

Instituto Butantã/Butantã Institute and Venomous animal and Museum ① *Av Dr Vital Brasil 1500, T011-3726 7222, Tue-Sun 0845-1615, www.butantan.gov.br, US$5, children half price under 12, under 7 free, Metrô Butantan (from 2012)*, on the university campus is one of the most popular tourist attractions in São Paulo. The Butantã Institute was founded at the start of the 20th century when Sao Paulo's governors looked to Brazilian scientists after an outbreak of bubonic plague in the port city of Santos. Over the decades, with Sao Paulo a booming centre of coffee production, researchers sought vaccines against snake bites to protect coffee harvesters working in the fields. The snakes are in pits and a large walk-through vivarium which also houses venomous spiders and scorpions. There is also a well-displayed, modern microbiology museum at the institute. The animals are milked for their venom six times a day and the antidotes have greatly reduced deaths from snakebite in Brazil. The centre also deals with spider and scorpion venom, has a small hospital and is a biomedical research institute responsible for producing about 90% of vaccines used in Brazil, including recent vaccines against H1N1 flu. Recent years have seen the institute invest in the hunt for natural vaccines in the Amazon rainforest. Visitors are not likely to see the venom being milked, but there is a museum of poisonous animals, which is well organized and educational, with explanations in Portuguese and English. The institute suffered a serious fire in May 2010, with the loss of the 85,000-strong preserved snake collection and 450,000 spider and scorpion specimens. It was the largest such collection in the world. The vivarium and public museum areas of the institute were not affected.

In the Prédio Novo da Reitoria, the **Museu de Arte Contemporânea (MAC)** ① *T011-3091 3039, www.mac.usp.br, Mon-Fri 1000-1800, Sun 1000-1600, free, Metrô Butantã (from 2012)*, has an important and beautifully presented collection of Brazilian and European modern art, with pieces by Braque, Picasso, Modigliani, Matisse and Tarsila do Amaral. Also in the university is the **Museu de Arqueologia e Etnologia (MAE)** ① *R Reitoria 1466, T011-3812 4001*, with an ill-kept collection of Amazonian and ancient Mediterranean material.

On the west bank of the Rio Pinheiros, just southeast of the campus, is the palatial **Jockey Club de São Paulo** ① *Av Lineu de Paula Machado 1263, T011-3811 7799*, a racecourse in the Cidade Jardim area. Race meetings are held on Monday and Thursday at 1930 and on weekends at 1430. The racecourse is easily accessible by bus from Praça da República.

Ipiranga and the Parque da Independência

① *To get to the park, take the Metrô to Alto do Ipiranga station, walk 30 m east to Av Dr Gentil de Moura and catch bus 478P-10 Sacoma-Pompeia to Av Nazaré (4 stops), get off and walk north for 200 m to the Parque da Independencia. It is also possible to catch the CPTM to Ipiranga station and walk east across the Viaduto Pacheco Chaves bridge and along R dos Patriotas (for 1 km). Bus No 478P (Ipiranga–Pompéia for return) runs from Metrô Ana Rosa and bus No 4612 from the Praça da República.*

The **Parque da Independência** ① *Av Nazare s/n, Metrô Alto de Ipiranga*, is a large, formal park on the site where Brazilian independence was declared, and littered with monuments to independence and Brazil's early Imperial past. It is watched over by a faux-French chateau, recalling Versailles, which houses one of the city's largest museums. Dominating the northern end of the park is the **Monumento à Independência**, depicting the first Brazilian Emperor, Dom Pedro, brandishing a furled flag and uttering his famous 'Grito de Ipiranga' (Ipiranga cry) – 'Independence or Death!', which declared Brazil's separation from

Portugal. Beneath the monument is the **imperial chapel** ⓘ *Tue-Sun 1300-1700*, containing Dom Pedro and Empress Leopoldina's tomb. The monument was built to commemorate the centenary of Independence in 1922. The **Casa do Grito** ⓘ *Tue-Sun 0930-1700*, is a replica of the tiny house where Dom Pedro I spent the night before uttering his grito. At that time, Ipiranga was outside the city's boundaries, in a wooded area on the main trade route between Santos and São Paulo. Bricks were made here from a local red clay called Ipiranga – in the Tupi language. This clay has given its name to the surrounding neighbourhood.

The **Museu Paulista** ⓘ *T011-2065 8000, www.mp.usp.br, Tue-Sun 0900-1645, US$2*, is housed in a huge palace at the top of the park. The original building, later altered, was the first monument to Independence. The museum contains old maps, traditional furniture, collections of old coins, religious art and rare documents, and has a department of indigenous ethnology. Behind the museum is the **Horto Botânico/Ipiranga Botanical Garden** ⓘ *Tue-Sun 0900-1700*, and the **Jardim Francês**, designed as a garden for plant study, now a recreational area. There is a light and sound show on Brazilian history in the park on Wednesday, Friday and Saturday at 2030.

Mooca and the Zona Leste

São Paulo's Zona Leste is predominantly a blue collar residential region that becomes progressively poorer the farther from the centre you go, eventually tailing off into vast sprawling favelas, like the Favela do Sapo, on the city's outskirts. Most of the city's domestic workers live here (or in similar marginalized communities such as Paraisópolis in the north), near Ipiranga or Jardim Angela (in Capão Redondo in the city's far south). One of the few well to do neighbourhoods, **Mooca**, is home to the impressive **Memorial do Imigrante** ⓘ *R Visconde de Parnaíba 1316, Mooca, T011-2692 1866, www.memorial doimigrante.org.br, Tue-Sun 1000-1700, US$3, Metrô Bresser, from where an original 1912 tram runs to and from the museum during opening hours*, dedicated to the hundreds of thousands of Europeans who flooded into the country from the late 19th century to harvest coffee and work the plantations. Most came on government-funded programmes similar to the one pound pacakage which populated Australia with British emigrants in the 20th century. As many as 10,000 Germans, Italians, Ukrainians, Spanish and Portuguese came to Brazil every day from the arrival of the first boat in 1870 until the last at beginning of Second World War. They were housed and fed for free for eight days before being left to the mercy of often ruthless landowners who had only recently abandoned slavery. Treatment was often so bad that adverts were run in Europe advising people not to leave for Brazil. This museum tells little of that story, or of the African-Brazilians who were denied work in favour of Europeans, in what amounted to a kind of employment apartheid, but there are fascinating exhibits on life in the early 20th- century Brazil and the lifestyle of the first immigrants.

The suburbs

Parque Burle Marx

ⓘ *Av Dona Helena Pereira de Moraes 200, Morumbi, daily 0700-1900, CPTM Estação Granja Julieta or Metrô Santo Amara, and taxi (US$10, no buses and unsafe to walk)*, was designed by the famous landscape designer Burle Marx. It is the only place in the city where you can walk along trails in the *Mata Atlântica* (Atlantic rainforest), but it is unsafe after dark as it lies very close to Paraisópolis, the second largest favela in São Paulo (after Heliópolis).

Santo Amaro Dam

The **Brazilian Grand Prix** is staged at the **Autódromo de Interlagos** ⓘ *Av Senador Teotônio Vilela 261, Interlagos, T011-5666 8822, www.autodromointerlagos.com*, overlooking a vast artificial lake set in remnant forest in the far southeast of the city. There are races all year round – with details of prices and what's on on the website. For information on the Brazilian Grand Prix. São Paulo merges with the beautiful misty mountains and cloud forests of the Serra do Mar beyond Interlagos, its concrete gradually giving way to fresh air and trees. At **Parelheiros** there is access to the the **Mata Atlântica** Atlantic coastal rain, cloud and elfin forests in and around the **Parque Estadual Serra do Mar**, a state park and protected area offering wonderful day hiking and excellent birdwatching. Maned wolf and ocelot still live in the area and brown capuchin monkeys are a common sight.

Paranapiacaba

ⓘ *Suburban trains leave from the Estação da Luz every 15 mins for Rio Grande da Serra (Line 10 – the turquoise line), US1.50, 55 mins. From Rio Grande da Serra station, bus No 424 runs to Paranapiacaba hourly during the week, every 30 mins at weekends. The journey is around 1 hr. A tourist train is schelduled to run hourly from Estação da Luz on Sun from 2011 – see www.cptm.sp.gov.br/e_operacao/exprtur/parana.asp for the latest details.*

This tiny 19th-century town, nestled in the cloudforest of the Serra do Mar about 50 km southeast of São Paulo, was built by English railway workers who constructed the São Paulo–Santos railway. Almost all of the houses are made of wood and many look like they belong in suburban Surrey. There is a small railway museum and a handful of little *pousadas* and restaurants. It is easily visited in a day trip from São Paulo.

The Serra da Cantareira

Whilst the Serra do Mar mountains bring greenery to São Paulo's southern edges, the Serra da Cantareira provides fresh air and forest to its north. Unlike the Serra do Mar, the Serra da Cantareira is cut by small roads, and at weekends Paulistanos traditionally love to slip on their Timberlands, climb into the car and drive through the hills in search of nothing wilder than a steakhouse. But there are trails, and if you're prepared to walk you can get lost in some semi-wilderness. It's best to go with a guide – through local company **Tropico**, www.tropico.tur.br, who offer guided hikes to rushing rainforest waterfalls with glassy plunge pools, and to boulder mountains with sweeping views of the skyscraper city over a canopy of trees.

São Paulo listings

For Sleeping and Eating price codes and other relevant information, see pages 10-13.

Sleeping

São Paulo has the best hotels in Latin America and by far the best city hotels in Brazil. There are designer hotels that Ian Shrager would be proud of, including business towers that combine all the requisite facilities with an almost personal touch. However, rooms are expensive and while there are some reasonable budget options they are not in the best locations. Sampa (as São Paulo is affectionately known) is a place where you have to spend money to enjoy yourself. The best places to stay are **Jardins** (the most affluent area) and on and around **Av Paulista** (close to one of the business centres). Backpackers should consider **Vila Madalena** – a lively nightlife centre with a recently opened hostel. Business travellers will find good hotels on **Faria Lima** and **Av Luís Carlos Berrini** (in the new centre in the south of the city). Some of the better hostels are in seemingly random locations and there are cheap options in the seedy centre, which is an undesirable place to be at night.

Centro Histórico *p25, map p26*
Metrô República and Anhangabaú

The city centre is very busy during the day but decidedly sketchy after dark. Consider taking a cab from your hotel door and be extra careful if you resolve to walk around. Be sure to book rooms on upper floors of hotels, preferably not facing the street for a quiet night in the city centre.

$$$ Marabá, Av Ipiranga 757, T011-2137 9500, www.maraba.com.br. By far the best small hotel in the city centre, this newly refurbished building has colourful, well-appointed modern rooms with concessions to boutique hotel design. The hotel has a small but cosy bar, a restaurant and a pocket-sized gym. Metrô República is a few mins' walk.

$$$ Novotel Jaraguá Convention, R Martins Fontes 71, T011-2802 7000, www.novotel.com. This freshly refurbished chain hotel with Wi-Fi in all rooms is the only business hotel of quality in the old centre. It sits in a convenient location right off Av 9 de Julho (with fast taxi access to the airports and business districts) and R Augusta (for Av Paulista), 5 mins' walk from Metrô Anhangabaú. The hotel has a convention centre and a large exhibition and lounge space in the marble lobby, bright, no-nonsense rooms in white and blonde wood with sturdy wooden workplaces a fresh bathrooms, a gym and disabled access to some rooms.

$$ Itamarati, Av Dr Vieira de Carvalho 150, T011-3474 4133, www.hotelitamarati.com.br. This long-standing cheapie is popular with budget travellers and represents the best value for money of any hotel in the city centre. The rooms are simple white cubes with little more than a bed, Brazilian TV, retro (or just antique) fridges, a small desk and a wardrobe, and the whole building has seen better days, but the location is excellent – just over 100 m from the EMTU airport bus stop and Metrô República.

$ Formule 1, Av São João 1140, Centre, just off Praça da República, T011-6878 6400, www.accor.com.br. With pre-payment and short shrift service, you'll feel like you're part of a process rather than a guest at this tall chain hotel tower. However, the modern, functional and anonymous little a/c boxes they sell as rooms are spick and span and come with en suites, TVs, work places and space for up to 3 people. 5 mins' walk from Metrô República.

Avenida Paulista and Jardins *p32 and p34, maps p22 and p34*
Metrô Brigadeiro, Trianon MASP, Consolação and Oscar Freire (under construction)

These plush neighbourhoods are among the safest in the city and offer easy walking access to São Paulo's finest restaurants, cafés, and shops. Those close to Av Paulista are a stroll from one of a string of metrô stations. A new metrô is under construction at R Oscar Freire (due 2012-2013) in the heart of Jardins.

$$$$ Emiliano, R Oscar Freire 384, T011-3069 4369, www.emiliano.com.br. Together with the **Fasano** and **Unique**, these are best suites in the city: bright, light and beautifully designed with attention to every detail. No pool but a relaxing small spa. Excellent Italian restaurant, location and service.

$$$$ Fasano, R Vittorio Fasano 88, T011-3896 4077, www.fasano.com.br. One of the world's great hotels. There's a fabulous pool, a spa and the best formal haute-cuisine restaurant in Brazil. The lobby bar is a wonderful place to arrange a meeting. Excellent position in Jardins.

$$$$ George V, R Jose Maria Lisboa 1000, T011-3088 9822, www.george-v.com.br. This tower block in the heart of Jardins offers some of the largest rooms in central São Paulo – albeit with dull Argos-like furnishings. Apartments cover 60-180 sq m, with living rooms, fully equipped kitchens (with dishwashers and washing machines), huge bathrooms, closets and comprehensive business services. Shared facilities include sauna, indoor pool and modern gym. Special deals available on the website.

$$$$ L'Hotel, Av Campinas 266, T011-2183 0500, www.lhotel.com.br. Part of the **Leading Hotels of the World** group, with a series of suites decorated with mock-European paintings and patterned wallpaper, in emulation of the classic hotel look of New York's Upper East Side. The St Regis this is not, but it's comfortable, intimate, offers good,

discreet service and a respectable French restaurant and it's a convenient base for Paulista.

$$$$ Renaissance, Alameda Santos 2233 (at Haddock Lobo), T011-3069 2233, www.marriott.com. This tall tower designed by Ruy Ohtake is the best business hotel for business around Av Paulista, with spacious and well-appointed rooms (the best with wonderful city views), a good spa, gym, pool and 2 squash courts. There are excellent business and conference facilities including a full business centre, secretarial services and airline booking and Wi-Fi comes in all areas.

$$$$ Unique, Av Brigadeiro Luís Antônio 4700, Jardim Paulista, T011-3055 4700, www.hotel unique.com. The most ostentatiously designed hotel in the country: an enormous half moon on concrete uprights with curving floors, circular windows and beautiful use of space and light. The bar on the top floor is São Paulo's answer to the LA Sky Bar and is filled with the beautiful and famous.

$$$$ Tivoli Mofarrej, R Alameda Santos 1437, Jardins, T011-3146 5900, www.tivolihotels.com. A selection of plush, modern carpeted suites and smaller rooms, the best of which are on the upper storeys and have superb city views. The hotel has the best spa in the city – run by the Banyan Tree group, a pool, business facilities, free Wi-Fi and a well-equipped gym. Service is patchy, however, and beware of making phone calls from the rooms – they are very expensive.

$$$ Golden Tulip Park Plaza, Alameda Lorena 360, T011-2627 6000, www.goldentulippark plaza.com. Modern tower with apartments of 30 sq m, spa, worn-out gym and internet. Rooms are in desperate need of a re-vamp. The location is excellent – safe and with easy walking access to Jardins restaurants and Paulista. Good views from the upper storeys.

$$$ Transamérica Ópera, Alameda Lorena 1748, T011-3062 2666, www.transamerica

flats.com.br. Conservatively decorated but elegant and well-maintained modern flats of 42 sq m in a tower between the heart of Jardins and Av Paulista. At the bottom end of this price range. Gym, free Wi-Fi, parking and room service.

$$ Estan Plaza, Alameda Jau 497, Jardins, T011-3016 0000, www.estanplaza.com.br. Well-kept, simple and pocket-sized rooms in a well-situated tower block close to both the restaurants of Jardins and to Av Paulista. Rooms are at a similar price to hostel doubles making this excellent value.

$$ Ibis São Paulo Paulista, Av Paulista 2355, T011-3523 3000, www.accorhotels. com.br. Great value. Modern, business-standard rooms with a/c in a tower right on Av Paulista. Cheaper at weekends. Online reservations.

$$ Landmark Residence, Alameda Jaú 1607, T011-3082 8600, www.landmarkresidence. com.br. Spacious apartments with tired catalogue furnishings (saggy sofas, uninspiring wall prints), broadband in all rooms, a gym, gardens and a modest business centre. The location, however, is excellent – with easy walking to the chic shops, cafés and restaurants.

$$ Paulista Garden, Alameda Lorena 21, T/F011-3885 8498, www.paulistagardenhotel. com.br. Small, simple wooden rooms with a/c, cable TV and fridges but no workspaces. 10 mins' walk uphill to Paulista (for Brigadeiro Metrô), 15 to Ibirapuera park and 20 to the heart of Jardins. There are plenty of restaurants nearby and the area is safe. Tiny gym and rooftop patio with a view.

$$ Pousada Dona Zilah, Alameda Franca 1621, Jardim Paulista, T011-3062 1444, www.zilah. com. Little *pousada* in a renovated colonial house with plain but well-maintained rooms and common areas decorated with thought and a personal touch. Excellent location, bike rental and generous breakfast included. Triple rooms available (**$**).

Vila Madalena and Pinheiros *p36, map p22*
Metrô Vila Madalena and Pinheiros (under construction)

These are a great neighbourhoods to stay in – with a wealth of little shops, café-restaurants, bars and nightclubs. The metrô station is 10 mins' walk from most of the action but there are fast subway trains from here to the city centre and connections to Paulista and the *rodoviária*. There are only 2 accommodation options for now. But more will surely come.

$$ Casa Club, R Mourato Coelho 973, T011 3798 0051, www.casaclub.com.br. There are only 4 rooms in this tiny hostel and whilst they're all dorms they can be booked as private rooms – hence the price discrepancy. One is for women only. The hostel began life as a bar and the after-hours party atmosphere remains to this day, so its not an option for those craving peace or privacy. Free Wi-Fi and a restaurant.

$$ Sampa Hostel, R Girassol 519, T011- 3031 6779, www.hostelsampa.com.br. This small hostel is in the heart of Vila Madalena, close to shops, cafés and bars. The 2 private rooms fill up quickly so book ahead, the rest of the accommodation is in dorms. All are fan cooled. Prices include breakfast. Wi-Fi is available throughout the hostel at a flat one-off US$3.50 fee.

South of the Centre *p36, map p22*
Metrô Anhangabaú, Liberdade, Paraíso and Vergueiro

$$ 3 Dogs Hostel, R Cel Artur Godoi 51, Vila Mariana, T011-2359 8222, www.3dogs hostel.com.br. Double rooms and dorms, breakfast and bed linen included, with garden and free Wi-Fi.

$$ Formule 1, R Vergueiro 1571, T011- 5085 5699, www.accorhotels.com.br. Another great-value business-style hotel, with a/c apartments big enough for 3 (making this an **$** option for those in a group). Right next to Paraíso Metrô in a safe area.

$$ Pousada dos Franceses, R dos Franceses 100, Bela Vista, T011-3288 1592, www.pousadadosfranceses.com.br. Price per person. A plain little *pousada* with an attractive garden, a BBQ area, laundry facilities, dorms, doubles and singles. 10 mins' walk from Brigadeiro Metrô. Free internet, TV room and breakfast included.

$$ Praça da Árvore IYHA, R Pageú 266, Saúde, T011-5071 5148, www.spalbergue.com.br. This pleasant little hostel with friendly, helpful (and English-speaking staff) lies 2 mins from the Praça do Arvore Metrô – some 20 mins' ride from the city centre. It is situated in a large residential house in a quiet back street. Facilities include a kitchen, laundry and internet service.

$$ Vergueiro Hostel, R Vergueiro 434, Liberdade, T011-2649 1323, www.hostel vergueiro.com. This 2009 opening has simple eggshell blue or burnt ochre rooms with parquet wood or square-tile floors, some of which have balconies. Studio apartments come with either double beds or 3 singles and shared rooms have 6 beds in wooden bunks. Rooms have private bathrooms, there is free Wi-Fi and breakfast is included.

Itaim Bibi, Vila Olímpia and Moema
p39, map p22

Metrô Faria Lima (from 2012), CPTM Vila Olímpia and Cidade Jardim

$$$$ Blue Tree Towers, Av Brigadeiro Faria Lima 3989, Vila Olímpia, T011-3896 7544, www.bluetree.com.br. Modern business hotel with discreetly designed rooms and excellent service. Ideally positioned for Faria Lima's business district and the restaurants and night-life of Vila Olímpia and Itaim. Pool, massage, gym, sauna and well-equipped business centre.

Brooklin and the New Business District *p39, map p22*
This is São Paulo's new business capital. Most hotels are to be found on Av Brigadeiro Faria Lima and Av Luís Carlos Berrini.

$$$$ Grand Hyatt São Paulo, Av das Nações Unidas 13301, T011-2838 1234, www.saopaulo.hyatt.com. A superb business hotel close to Av Luís Carlos Berrini, which successfully fuses corporate efficiency and requisite services with designer cool. Spa, pool, state-of-the-art business centre and marvellous views from the upper-floor suites.

$$$$ Hilton São Paulo, Av das Nações Unidas 12901, T011-2845 0000, www.hilton.com. This tall tower in the heart of the new business district overlooks the new Octavio Frias de Oliveira twin suspension bridge and boasts a vast marble lobby with Wi-Fi access (none in rooms), business and conference facilities and a 24-hr spa. Rooms come with marble bathrooms, an office workstation with broadband and sweeping city views from the upper floors. Suites have separate living rooms, kitchenettes and a second bathroom with Jacuzzin and a TV.

The suburbs *p41*
$$$$ Unique Garden Spa, Estrada 3500, Serra da Cantareira, T011-4486 8724, www.unique garden.com.br. The über-cool style of hotel **Unique** (see page 44) transposed into a natural setting of the Serra da Cantareira subtropical forest, 40 mins north of São Paulo. The buildings are equally impressive, with Ruy Ohtake's iron-grey post-industrial half-moon replaced with a series of Frank Lloyd Wright-inspired post-modernist bungalows. The spa treatments are wonderful. Shuttles can be organized through hotel **Unique**.

❷ Eating

Those on a budget can eat to their stomach's content in per kilo places or, if looking for cheaper still, in *padarias* (bakeries). There is one of these on almost every corner. They all serve sandwiches such as *Misto Quentes*, *Beirutes* and *Americanos* – delicious Brazilian burgers made from decent meat and served with ham, egg, cheese or salad. They always have good coffee, juices, cakes and *almoços* (set lunches) for a very economical price. Most have a designated seating area, either at the *padaria* bar or in an adjacent room; you aren't expected to eat on your feet as you are in Rio. Restaurants in São Paulo are safe on the stomach. Juices are made with mineral or filtered water.

Centro Histórico *p25, map p26*
Metrô Luz, República, São Bento, Anhangabaú, Sé

You are never far from a café or restaurant in the city centre and Luz. The Pinacoteca galleries, the Centro Culutral Banco do Brasil and the Pátio de Colégio all have decent cafés, and there are dozens in the streets around the Mosteiro São Bento and the Teatro Municipal. Most tend to be open during lunchtime only and there are many per kilo options and *padarias*.

¶¶¶ Terraço Italia, Av Ipiranga 344, T011-3257 6566. An overpriced Italian restaurant, with stodgy pasta, lukewarm risottos and a huge menu of very mediocre pan-European food and the best views in the city of any dining room in São Paulo. Come for a coffee only, although there's a minimum charge of US$12.

Luz *p30, map p22*
¶¶-¶ Café da Pinacoteca, Pinacoteca Museum, Praça da Luz 2, Luz, T011-3326 0350. This Portuguese-style café with marble floors and mahogany balconies overlooks the Parque da Luz on the basement floor of the Pinacoteca gallery. It serves great coffee, sandwiches, snacks and cakes. There is also a café of similar quality in the Estação Pinacoteca gallery.

¶¶-¶ Ponto Chic, Largo do Paiçandu 27, T011-3222 6528; www.pontochic.com.br. Paulistanos rave about this rather unprepossessing little corner café in the heart of the city. A slice of Brazilian culinary history, the *Bauru* sandwich was born here in 1922. A bronze bust of Casemiro Pinto Neto, who apparently first conceived the groundbreaking idea of combining cheese, salad and roast beef in a French bread roll, adorns the back wall. The sandwich itself has a page of the menu devoted to its history, but arrives with little ceremony on a plain white plate, overflowing with gooey cheese and thick with fine-cut beef.

Barra Funda and Higienópolis *p32, map p22*

¶¶¶ AK Delicatessan, R Mato Grosso 450, Higienópolis, T011-3231 4497. After moving back to her native São Paulo from New York, former film-producer Andrea Kaufmann resolved to open a New York style deli and an upstairs restaurant decorated with strips of retro wall paper and dedicated to Jewish home cooking. Dishes include Eastern European veal goulash with spätzle, pearl onions and sour cream and, in the deli, warm bagels and pastrami. The restaurant has won numerous awards, including the Folha de São Paulo restaurant-of-the-year award.

¶¶¶ Anita, R Mato Grosso 154, T011-2628 3584, www.restauranteanita.com.br. Simple but elegantly prepared comfort food in this little restaurant next to the AK Delicatessan. Lunchtime is especially popular when fashionable 20-something girls pull up here to lunch on filet mignon or linguini with mushrooms and cracked pepper, after spending the morning browsing in nearby Jardins.

¶¶¶ Carlota, R Sergipe 753, Higienópolis, T011- 3661 8570, www.carlota.com.br. Chef Carla Pernambuco was a pioneer of fine dining in Brazil when she first opened her restaurant in the mid-1990s. Her recipe of unpretentious, homey surrounds, warm service and Brazilian and Mediterranean fusion cooking has been copied by numerous others in São Paulo. Dishes include fillet of grouper with plantain banana purée and fresh asparagus.

Avenida Paulista and Consolação *p32, map p34*

Metrô Consolação, Trianon-MASP, Brigadeiro.
Restaurants in this area lie along the course of Av Paulista or in the up-and-coming nightlife are of Consolação to its north. Jardins lies within easy access to the south.

♉♉♉ Spot, Av Ministro Rocha Azevedo 72, T011-3284 6131, www.restaurantespot.com.br. This chic São Paulo take on an American diner has been a favourite before-and-after club spot for fashionable Paulistanos for more than a decade. The wealthy, beautiful and well-dressed gather here to eat easy-on-the-waistline plates like grilled steak poivre, salmon with balsamic vinegar and seared tuna with soy and lime sauce.

♉♉ Sujinho, R da Consolação 2068 and 2063, Consolação, T011-3231 1299, www.sujinho.com.br. Burgers, pastas, salads, grilled fish, spit-roast chicken and sizzling meat all served in large portions. Home delivery available.

♉♉-♉ America, Av Paulista 2295, Consolação, T011-3067 4424, www.americaburger.com.br. This immensely popular a/c tribute to the New York diner and the North American burger is a great choice for families. Food comes quickly in Texan portions and with crisp waiter service. There are veggie options alongside the huge hunks of beef, a salad bar and a generous choice of sticky puddings and sugar-saturated shakes.

♉♉ Restaurante do MASP, Av Paulista 1578, T011-3253 2829 (see page 32). This bright, hospital clean buffet restaurant in the basement of the museum serves good-value comfort food such as lasagne and stroganoff, accompanied by salad from the buffet bar.

♉♉-♉ Fran's Café, Av Paulista 358, and all over the city. Open 24 hrs. Coffee chain serving aromatic, strong, richly flavoured coffee at a civilized temperature and in European-sized china cups, together with a menu of light eats.

Jardins *p34, map p34*

Metrô Oscar Freire (from 2013), Consolação or Trianon-MASP 10 mins' walk
Most of the city's fine dining restaurants lie in this upmarket grid of streets to the south of Av Paulista.

♉♉♉ Charlô Bistro, R Barão de Capanema 440 (next to **D.O.M**), T011-3087 4444, with another branch at the high-society set **Jockey Club**, Av Lineu de Paula Machado 1263, Cidade Jardim, T011-3034 3682. One of the premier VIP and old family haunts in the city. Decked out in tribute to a Paris brasserie and a menu of simple but elegant Mediterranean and fusion dishes such as Mediterranean squid with black rice and duck risotto with almonds and a curry sauce.

♉♉♉ Dalva e Dito, R Padre Joao Manoel 1115, T011-3064 6183, www.dalvaedito.com.br. Brazil's most internationally vaunted chef, Alex Atala, opened his new dining room in 2009 to serve Brazilian home cooking with a gourmet twist. Dishes include roast pork with pureed potato and catfish with aromatic capim-santo grass from the plains of the Brazilian interior. A long open kitchen cuts through the middle of the bright, soaring dining room. The food is better value than it is in D.O.M and the atmosphere more familial.

♉♉♉ D.O.M, R Barão de Capanema 549, T011-3088 0761. This has been Jardins' evening restaurant of the moment for almost a decade. The kitchen is run by chef Alex Attala, who has won the coveted *Veja* award several times. Contemporary food fuses Brazilian ingredients with French and Italian styles and is served in a large, open, modernist dining room to the sharply dressed.

♉♉♉ Dui, Alameda Franca 1590, T011-2649 7952, www.duirestaurante.com.br. Sumptuous, light Brazilian-Asian-Mediterranean fusion. Great cocktails in the downstairs bar.

♉♉♉ Eñe, R Dr Mario Ferraz 213, T011-3816 4333, www.enerestaurante.com.br. Brazil's foremost modern Spanish restaurant is helmed by Sergio and Javier Torres Martínez who have worked with Alain Ducasse and Josep Lladonosa of the Escola Arnadí. The *degustação* is a smorgasbord of Spanish and Brazilian-inspired tapas with choices such as breaded mussels with cream of white carrot with tapioca pearls. They come accompanied with the best choice of Spanish wines in Brazil.

¶¶¶ Fasano, Fasano Hotel (see Sleeping), R Fasano, T011-3062 4000, www.fasano.com.br. The flagship restaurant of the Fasano group has long been regarded as the best restaurant for gourmets in São Paulo. The menu offers a huge choice of modern Italian and French cooking, modelled on the best of Milan from chef Salvatore Loi and served in a magnificent room where diners have their own low-lit booths and are served by flocks of black-tie waiters. The wine list is exemplary and the dress formal dress.

¶¶¶ Figueira Rubaiyat, R Haddock Lobo 1738, T011-3063 1399, www.rubaiyat.com.br. The most interesting of the **Rubaiyat** restaurant group, with steaks prepared by Brazilian chef, Francisco Gameleira. Very lively for lunch on a Sun and remarkable principally for the space: open walled, light and airy and shaded by a huge tropical fig tree.

¶¶¶ Gero, R Haddock Lobo 1629, T011-3064 0005, www.fasano.com.br. Fasano's version of a French bistro serves pasta and light Italian food in carefully designed, casually chic surrounds. The evening clientele includes some of the best-known and most expensively reconstructed faces in São Paulo high society – making this a prime spot for people-watching, but be prepared for a long wait at the bar alongside people who are there to be seen. No reservations.

¶¶¶ La Tambouille, Av 9 de Julho 5925, Jardim Europa, T011-3079 6277, www.tambouille.com.br. The favourite fusion restaurant of the city's old-money society. Chef Giancarlo Bolla, a native of San Remo in northern Italy, learnt his trade on the Italian Riviera and prepares dishes like fillet of sole with passion fruit sauce served with banana and shrimp farofa and filet mignon wrapped in parma ham and cooked in red wine and served with brie ravioli. Excellent wine list. The restaurant offers a good-value three course gourmet lunch Tue-Fri.

¶¶¶ Massimo, Alameda Santos 1826, Cerqueira César, T011-3284 0311. One of São Paulo's longest-established Italian restaurants serving simple northern Italian dishes and a wide selection of very fresh, grilled seafish to the city's politicians and business executives. The wine list stretches to 100 bottles and credit cards are not accepted, despite the elevated price.

¶¶¶-¶¶ Marakuthai, Alameda Itu 1618, T011-3061 1015, www.marakuthai.com.br. A Paulistano take on Indian and Southeast Asian food. Dishes are Brazilian experiments with Asian ingredients.

¶¶ A Mineira, Alameda Joaquim Eugenio de Lima 697, T011-3283 2349. This self-service restaurant offers Minas food by the kilo from a buffet which sizzles in earthenware pots over a woodfire stove. There's plenty of choice and a small draft of *Cachaça* and desserts are included in the price.

¶¶ Baalbek, Alameda Lorena 1330, T011-3088 4820. Lebanese cooking, with great falafel, Arabic salads and sweet desserts. Closed in the evenings.

¶¶ Kayomix, R da Consolação 3215, T011-3082 2769. Brazilian-Oriental fusions with dishes such as salmon taratare with shimeji and shitake.

¶¶ Sattva, Alameda Itu 1564, T011-3083 6237, www.sattvanatural.com.br. Light vegetarian curries, stir fries, salads, pizzas and pastas all made with organic ingredients. There is a great-value dish of the day lunchtime menu on weekdays and live music most nights.

¶¶ Santo Grão, R Oscar Freire 413, T011-3082 9969, www.santograo.com.br. This smart café with tables spilling out onto the street is a favourite coffee and cakes or light lunch stop for wealthy society shoppers. The coffee is superb, freshly roasted and comes in a number of varieties.

Cheiro Verde, R Peixoto Gomide 1078, Jardins, T011-3262 2640 (lunch only), www.cheiroverderestaurante.com.br. Hearty vegetarian food, such as vegetable crumble in gorgonzola sauce and wholewheat pasta with buffalo mozzarella and sundried tomato.

Vila Madalena and Pinheiros *p36, map p22*

The streets of Vila Madalena are lined with restaurants and cafés – many on **Aspicuelta** and **Girassol**. Most of the bars and clubs serve food too, and some – such as **Grazie o Dio!** – have designated restaurants. Pinheiros has some of the best fine dining restaurants in the city.

Jun Sakamoto, R Lisboa 55, Pinheiros, T011-3088 6019. Japanese cuisine with a French twist. Superb fresh ingredients, some of it flown in especially from Asia and the USA. The dishes of choice are the degustation menu and the duck breast teppaniyaki.

Mani, R Joaquim Antunes 210, Pinheiros, T011-3085 4148. Superior light Mediterranean menu, which utilizes Brazilian ingredients and perfectly complements the waistlines of the celebrity crowd. Daniel Redondo and partner Helena Rizzo have worked in Michelin-starred restaurants in Europe.

Deli Paris, R Harmonia 484, Vila Madalena, T011-3816 5911, www.deliparis.com.br. This Paulistano homage to a French café serves light and flavourful sweet and savoury crepes, sickly sweet petit gateaux au chocolat, cheese-heavy quiches, salads and crunchy sandwiches to a busy lunchtime and evening crowd.

Genial, R Girassol 374, T011-3812 7442. This bar, with a black and white mosaic floor and black-tie waiters, is decorated with LP covers by famous traditional musicians such as João do Vale and Luiz Gonzaga. The *chope* is creamy and best accompanied by a *petisco* bar snack – like *caldinho de feijão* (bean broth) or *bolinhos de bacalhau* (codfish balls), both of which are among the best in Vila Madalena. There's a hearty and very popular *feijoada* on Sat and Sun lunch.

South of the Centre *p36, map p22*

Liberdade is dotted with Japanese restaurants and has a lively market on Sun with plenty of food stalls. Bela Vista is replete with Italian restaurants, most of them rather poor – with stodgy pasta and gooey risotto. Ibirauera Park has lots of mobile snack bars selling ice cream, sugar cane juice, hot dogs and snacks, and there is a good-value buffet restaurant close to the Museu Afro Brasileiro.

Famiglia Mancini, R Anhandava, T011-3255 6599, www.famigliamancini.com.br. This pretty little pedestrianized street 10 mins' walk from the Terraço Italia is lined with Italian restaurants and delicatessans, almost all of them in the locally owned Famiglia Mancini group. Here, the big dining room with formal waiters and an enormous menu of meats, pastas, risottos, fish and (inevitably for São Paulo) pizzas, is the family's flagship restaurant. Walls are lined with the faces of famous Brazilians who have dined here. The restaurant is very busy with families on weekends and reservations are necessary.

Aska Lámen, R Galvão Buemno 466, Liberadade, T011-3277 9682. One of Liberadade's more traditional Japanese restaurants with a bar overlooking an open kitchen where chefs serve piping ramen noodle dishes to lunchtime diners who are 90% *issei* (Japonese immigrants and their descendants).

Prêt, Museu de Arte Moderna (MAM), Parque Ibirapuera, T011-5574 1250, www.mam.org.br. Closed evenings. This lunchtime buffet serves the best food in the park – ultra-fresh pre-prepared soups, salads, chicken, fish, meat and vegetarian dishes. It sits in a semi-circular dining room at the front of MAM, bathed in light from 3-m-high glass windows and looking out over the sculpture garden and Niemeyer's Oca. The Bienal building (for Fashion Week and the Art shows) is less than 200 m away.

†† Gombe, R Tomás Gonzaga 22, T011-3209 8499. Renowned for ultra-fresh seared tuna and steaming hot udon and ramen dishes.

†† Sushi Yassu, R Tomas Gonzaga 98, T011-3288 2966, www.sushiyassu.com.br. The best of Liberdade's traditional Japanese restaurants with a large menu of sushi/sashimi combinations, teishoku (complete set meals with cooked and raw dishes) and very sweet Brazilianized desserts.

Itaím, Vila Olímpia and Moema *p39, map p22*

These areas, south of the centre, have dozens of ultra-trendy restaurants with beautiful people posing in beautiful surroundings. We include only a handful of the best.

††† 348 Parrilla Porteña, R Comendador Miguel Calfat, 348, Vila Olímpia, T011- 3849 0348, www.restaurante348.com.br. An Argentinian restaurant with the best steak in the country from the choicest cuts available only on export from Buenos Aires. The *ojo del bife* cuts like brie and collapses in the mouth like wafered chocolate. The accompanying wines are equally superb, especially the 2002 Cheval dos Andes. Great, unpretentious atmosphere.

††† JAM Warehouse, R Lopes Neto 308, Itaim, T011-3473 3273, www.jamwarehouse.com.br. Japanese restaurant serving Japanese food with a Brazilian twist – with grilled and seared tuna and salmon, sushi stuffed with foie gras and cream cheese and sweet sushi dishes for dessert. There's more style than substance to the cooking, but the atmosphere is congenial, with live music every night and there's always a smart 'A' list crowd eager to be ogled.

††† Kinoshita, R Jacques Félix 405, Vila Nova Conceição, T011-3849 6940, www.restaurantekinoshita.com.br. Tsuyoshi Murakami offers the best menu of traditional cooked or Kappo cuisine in Brazil, dotted with creative fusion dishes in a Nobu vein. His cooking utilizes only the freshest ingredients and includes a sumptuous degustation menu with delights such as tuna marinated in soya, ginger and garlic, served with ponzo sauce and garnished with Kaiware (sprouted daikon radish seeds). Murakami trained in the ultra-traditional 100-year-old **Ozushi** restaurant in Shambashi Tokyo, **Shubu Shubu** in New York and **Kyokata** in Barcelona.

††† Kosushi, R Viradouro 139, Itaim Bibi and in Shopping Cidade Jardim, T011-3167 7272, www.kosushi.com.br. The first of São Paulo's chic Japanese restaurants, which began life in Liberdade and is now housed in a beautifully designed Asian modernist space. The rich and famous come here to be seen eating chef George Yuji Koshoji's huge sushi and sashimi combinations.

††† Parigi, R Amauri 275, Itaim, T011-3167 1575, www.fasano.com.br. One of the premier places to be seen; celebrity couples come here for intimate, public-view Franco-Italian dining. The menu also has classical French dishes such as *coq au vin*. Attractive dining room, beautifully lit, and decked out in lush dark wood.

Bars, clubs and live music

São Paulo has more nocturnal panache than Rio. There is great live music on most nights of the week. Large concert venues, such as the **Pacaembu Stadium**, host the likes of U2 or Ivete Sangalo. Medium-sized venues, such as **Credicard Hall**, are played by acts like Caetano Veloso, Gilberto Gil and Chico Buarque. Smaller venues include **SESCs** (cultural centres with excellent concert halls), and are found in Vila Mariana and Pompéia. They host smaller, classy artists such as Otto, Naná Vasconcelos, João Bosco and Seu Jorge.

It is also worth checking out the established smaller live venues in and around Vila Madalena and Itaim, such as **Bourbon St**, **A Marcenaria** and **Grazie a Dio** for samba-funk acts such as Tutti Baê and Funk como le Gusta, designated samba bars like **Ó do Borogodó** (also in Vila Madalena) and venues on the burgeoning alternative music scence, such as the **CB Bar** and **Studio SP** in Barra Funda and Consolação, respectively.

DJs like Marky and the sadly deceased Suba made the São Paulo club scene world famous, but gone are the days when Marky was resident DJ at the Lov.E Club and the city danced to homegrown sounds in clubs like Prime. São Paulo's sound systems and clubs are slicker and swankier than they have ever been, but the music is painfully derivative of New York and Europe.

The city has a bar at every turn – from spit-and-sawdust corner bars serving cold lager beer to an unpretentious blue-collar cord, to smarter mock-Portuguese *boteco* bars where penguin-suited waiters whirl around the tables brandishishing frothy glasses of draught lager or *chope* (pronounced 'chopee') and self-consciously chic cocktail bars where Paulistano high society flashes its jewels and flexes its pecs. Almost all serve food and many have live music. Beer and snacks are also available at the bar in any *padaria* (bakery).

Barra Funda *p32, map p22*
This dark and edgy neighbourhood northwest of Luz is gradually emerging as a new nightlife venue to rival Consolação. It's more Bohemian than the latter, with a sweep of bars and venues playing host to a bewildering variety of acts which have little to nothing in common beyond existing beyond the mainstream. It's not safe to walk around here after dark. Take the metrô and a cab.
Aldeia Turiassú, R Turiassú 928, T011- 3865 3055, www.aldeiaturiassu.com.br, http://bandagloria.com.br. On Fri this vast concert hall plays host to one of the best live samba gafieira acts in Brazil, Banda Glória, who play smoking dance-hall samba to a seething crowd of middle-class Paulistanos. 2 of the band's singers – Rubi and Andreia Dias – have become big names on São Paulo's alternative scene, signing up for record deals with cult record label Scubidy productions.
Bar do Alemão, Av Antártica 554, Água Branca, T011-3879 0070, http://bardo alemao.zip.net. This cosy little brick-walled bar and restaurant, on an ugly main road in a semi-residential quarter of Barra Funda, is famous for its live samba. There are samba shows most nights with an especially lively crowd at the weekends. Clara Nunes used to play here and famous samba musicians often appear still – including Paulo Cesar Pinheiro and Eduardo Gudin.
Berlin, R Cônego Vicente Miguel Marino 85, T011-3392 4594, www.clubeberlin.com.br. This cool, low-lit, long bar attracts an intelligent, arty crowd of 20- and 30-somethings, who gather from Tue-Sat to hear live contemporary Brazilian jazz with a psychedelic twist on Tue, Brazilian alternative and indie on Thu and pan-Latin American dance fusion on Fri.
CB, R Brigadeiro Galvão 871, T011-3666 8971, www.cbbar.com.br. This low-lit alternative rock and vanguarda venue is one of the best places in the city to hear interesting new acts. The line-up is eclectic, with local and out-of-state bands opening from Tue-Sat and alternating with Paulistano DJs.
D-Edge, Alameda Olga 170, T011-3667 8334, www.d-edge.com.br. This is one of the few São Paulo clubs to play Brazilian as well as international sounds. However, those searching for the shock of the new will still be disappointed by the homages to Ibiza and New York which dominate on most nights.
Pacha, R Mergenthaler 829, Vila Leopoldina, T011-2189 3700, www.pachasp.com.br. Those looking to come to São Paulo and experience Ibiza nightlife will love this gaudy

temple to Ibiza, with decks manned by the world's top DJs and dance floors packed with the city's wealthiest and most expensively clad. But with the US$1000 entrance fee to the VIP area, it would be cheaper for Europeans at least to opt for the real thing in Ibiza. Those without a Dubai prince's urge to be seen to spend can enter the dance area, reserved for the hoy poloy, for a 20th of the price.

SESC Pompeia, R Clélia, 93. Pompéia, T011-3871 7700, ww.sesccsp.org.br. There's always a great show at this arts and cultural centre in the neighbouring bairro to Barra Funda. Some of Brazil's best small acts play at weekends.

The Week, R Guaicurus 324, Barra Funda, T011-3872 9966, www.theweek.com.br. One of the city's biggest gay- and lesbian-dominated dance clubs, whose party to attend is Babylon (in the VIP room on Sat nights). It's packed with pill-popping gym bodies gyrating to progressive trance. There are a further 6000 sq m of dance floor and there's even a pool for when it all gets too hot.

Avenida Paulista and Consolação *p32, map p34*

Until a few years ago the dark streets of Consolação were home to little more than rats, sleazy strip bars, street-walkers and curb-crawlers, but now it harbours a thriving alternative weekend scene. Shortly after R Augusta crosses Av Paulista from Jardins, it leaves the smart and swanky for a mish-mash of untidy streets, grafitti-scrawled shop fronts broken by the deep velvet-red of open bar doors. Go-go clubs with heavy-set bouncers loitering outside sit alongside makeshift street bars where a jostle of hundreds of young Paulistanos down bottles of Bohemia beer at rickety metal tables or brush aside their emo fringes as they queue to enter a gamut of fashionable bars, clubs and pounding gay venues.

Clube Royal, R Consolação 222, T011-3129 9804, www.royalclub.com.br. One of the most fashionable funk and rare groove clubs on the young and need-to-be-seen São Paulo circuit is decorated like a New York dive bar in Brazilian tropical colours. Celebrities who choose to dance here include Gisele Bundchen and the hottest night are Desire and Shine on Fri and Sat respectively. Don't expect to hear any Brazilian music.

Hotel Cambridge, Av 9 de Julho 210, Centro, www.noitesdocentro.com.br /index.php? destino=cambridge. In the 1950s, the Cambridge was been a bastion of the city's bossa nova scene. Nowadays its frayed post-war deco provides the backdrop for alternative bands and DJs who gather here throughout the week but particularly on Fri and Sat to hear an assortment of bands.

Outs Club, R Augusta 486, T011-6867 6050, www.clubeouts.com. One of the bastions of the alternative, rock and hard rock scene with a mix of DJs playing everything from UK indie to heavy Brazilian metal bands.

Sonique, R Bela Cintra 461, Consolação, T011-2628 8707, www.soniquebar.com.br. The crowd in the neon-lit, high-ceilinged cavern of a room which comprises this club may look alternative but they are merely climbing on the grunge bandwagon. Whilst it's a great spot for people-watching, the club sounds are mainstream for anyone coming from Europe or the USA. The venue is intended as a warm-up for the larger clubs around town, with an airport-like messageboard announcing what is happening where.

Studio SP, R Augusta 591, T011-3129 7040, www.studiosp.org. A show hall on the neighbourhood's main thoroughfare. Turning up for the support act (usually before 2200) means getting in for free to see the main show. Bands like Trash pour Quatro, www.trashpour4.com, offer bossa nova re-workings of kitsch classics like *Material Girl*, in the spirit of Berk and the Virtual Band.

Singers such as Andreia Dias, www.andreia dias.com.br, offer smoky, seductive electronica mixed with lilting Brazilian rhythms. They intersperse with harder mangue beat acts like Mombojo from Pernambuco, www.mombojo.com.br.

Volt, R Haddock Lobo 40, Consolação, T011-2936 4041, www.barvolt.com.br. Just across Av Paulista from Consolação, a hip creative industry crowd sip fruit *batidas* to Brazilian drum and bass and Chicago house in this 400-sq-m space. It's lit with luminescent pink and green strip lights and decorated with a mirror wall, vertical fern garden and Eames wooden chairs and is a favourite pre- and post-club stop.

Vegas Club, R Augusta 765, T011-3231 3705, www.vegasclub.com.br. International and local DJs spin a predictable menu of techno, psi-trance and house to a mixed gay and straight crowd dancing on 2 sweaty floors from Tue-Sat.

Jardins *p34, map p34*

Bar Balcão, R Doutor Melo Alves 150, T011-3063 6091. After-work meeting place, very popular with young professionals and media types who gather on either side of the long low wooden bar, which winds its way around the room like a giant snake.

Barretto, in the **Fasano Hotel** (see Sleeping). A rather conservative atmosphere with heavy dark wood, mirrors and cool live bossa jazz. The crowd is mostly the Cuban cigar type with a sprinkling of the tanned and toned, in figure-enhancing designer labels.

Emiliano Bar, Emiliano Hotel (see Sleeping). Similar crowd to **Skye** but despite its popularity, it can feel like a sterile corridor rather than an intimate space. DJs play on Fri nights.

Dry Bar, R Padre João Manuel 700, T011-3729 6653, www.drybar.com.br. This low-lit, dark bar, with walls decorated with black pooltable balls, is a favourite with Jardins' rich, young and single, who throng here in the late evening to drink from a menu of more than a dozen dry martinis. The bar also serves excellent, expensive bar snacks.

Finnegan's Pub, R Cristiano Viana 358, Pinheiros, T011-3062 3232, www.finnegan. com.br. One of São Paulo's Irish bars. This one is actually run and owned by an Irishman and is very popular with expats.

Casa de Francisca, R José Maria Lisboa 190 at Brigadeiro Luís Antônio, T011-3493 5717, www.casadefrancisca.blogspot.com, This intimate, live music restaurant bar plays host to the refined end of the musical spectrum with acts such as virtuoso guitarist and composer Chico Saraiva, multi-instrumentalist Arthur de Faria or pianist Paulo Braga. The tables to book are those on the upper deck.

Skye, the rooftop bar at **Unique Hotel** (see Sleeping). Another fashionable spot with a definite door policy. The views of glistening skyscrapers pocked by patches of green and red tile are wonderful.

Mokai, R Augusta 2805, T011-3081 3103, www.mokai.com.br. This cool, concrete rectangle with headphones on the walls playing the latest club sounds from the world over, and dance floor lit by twinkling 550-sq-ft LED ceilings, is owned by Amir Slama (creator of Brazil's most internationally successful label, Rosa Chá) and his millionaire playboy friend Rico Mansur. There is a strict door policy. Dress down but well, book ahead through a concierge or someone pretending to be so, and enjoy the people-watching.

Vila Madalena and Pinheiros *p36, map p22*

Vila Madalena and adjacent Pinheiros lie just northeast of Jardins. A taxi from Jardins is about US$7; there is also a metrô station, but this closes by the time the bars get going. These suburbs are the favourite haunts of São Paulo 20-somethings, more hippy chic than Itaim, less stuffy than Jardins. This is the best part of town for live Brazilian music and uniquely Brazilian close dances such as *forró*, as opposed to international club sounds. It can feel grungy and informal but is buzzing. The liveliest streets are **Aspicuelta** and **Girassol**.

A Marcenaria, R Fradique Coutinho 1378, T011-3032 9006, www.amarcenaria.com.br. This is the Vila Madalena bar of choice for the young, single lovers of Brazilian rock who gather here from 2130; the dance floor fills up at around 2300.

Bambu, R Purpurina 272, Vila Madalena, T011-3031 2331, www.bambubrasi bar.com.br. A kind of backland desert jig called *forró* has everyone up and dancing in this slice of mock-Bahia, with live northeastern accordion and *zabumba* drum bands in the front room and a hippy middle-class student crowd downing industrial strength caipirinhas out back.

DiQuinta, R Baumann 1435, T011-5506 0100, www.diquinta.com.br. Mainstream medium-sized acts play here and at other venues in Vila Madalena such as **Grazie o Dio**. This club is one of the few to be busy on a Thu night.

Grazie a Dio, R Girassol 67, T011-3031 6568, www.grazieadio.com.br. The best bar in Vila Madalena to hear live music – there's a different band every night with samba on Sun. Great for dancing. Always packed.

Ó do Borogodó, R Horácio Lane 21, Vila Madalena, T011-3814 4087. It can be hard to track down this intimate club opposite the cemetery. It's in an unmarked house next to a hairdressers on the edge of Vila Madalena. The tiny dance hall is always packed with people between Wed and Sat. On Wed there's classic *samba canção* from retired cleaner Dona Inah who sings material from the likes of Cartola and Ataulfo Alves; and on other nights there's a varied programme of *choro*, *forró* and MPB from some of the best samba players in São Paulo.

Posto 6, R Aspicuelta 644, Vila Madalena, T011-3812 7831. An imitation Rio de Janeiro *boteco* with attractive crowds and backdrop of bossa nova and MPB. Busy from 2100.

Sub Astor, R Delfina 163, Vila Madalena, T011-3815 1364, www.subastor.com.br. This velvety mood-lit lounge bar looks like a film set from a David Lynch movie and is filled with mols, vamps and playboys from the upper echelons of São Paulo society. The cocktails are superb – especially the fruity caipirinhas, and there is no better place in the neighbourhood to see the Vanity Fair.

Itaím, Vila Olímpia and Moema *p39, map p22*

This area, just south of Ibirapuera and north of the new centre, is about US$10 by taxi from Jardins and US$15 from the centre, but well worth the expense of getting here. It is packed with street-corner bars, which are great for a browse. The bars here, although informal, have a style of their own, with lively and varied crowds and decent service. The busiest streets for a bar wander are **R Atilio Inocenti** near the junction of Av Juscelino Kubitschek and Av Brigadeiro Faria Lima, **Av Hélio Pellegrino** and **R Araguari**, which runs behind it.

3X4, R Bandeira Paulista 676, Itaim, T011- 2122 4051, www.3p4.com.br, This achingly chic place to be seen in owned by fashion impresario Amir Slama has furniture by Philippe Starck and photography by Brazilian Vogue snapper André Schiliró. It's nominally a restaurant, offering light Asian-Mediterranean cooking, but really a club. The dressed-up fashiony crowd, who are too waistline conscious to eat anything delightful to the palate, come here to dance after midnight.

Bourbon Street, R dos Chanés 127, Moema, T011-5095 6100, www.bournbonstreet. com.br. Great little club with acts like funkster Tutti Bae and international acts like BB King.

Columbia, R Estados Unidos 1570. Lively. **Hell's Club** downstairs. Opens 0400, techno, wild.

Disco, R Professor Atílio Inocennti 160, Itaim, T011-3078 0404, www.clubdisco.com.br. One of the city's plushest high-society discos and a favourite with leading socialites and models, especially during fashion week. The decor is by Isay Weinfeld who designed the Fasano, and the music standard Eurotrash and US club sounds.

Na Mata Café, R da Mata 70, Itaim, T011-3079 0300, www.namata.com.br. Popular flirting and pick-up spot for 20- and 30-something rich kids who gyrate in the dark dance room to a variety of Brazilian and European dance tunes and select live bands.

Entertainment

São Paulo p20, maps p22, p26 and p34
For listings of concerts, theatre, museums, galleries and cinemas visit www.guiasp.com.br, or look in the *Guia da Folha* section of *Folha de São Paulo*, and the *Veja São Paulo* section of the weekly news magazine *Veja*.

Art galleries
Casa da Fazenda, Morumbi, exhibits in 19th-century house. **Espaço Cultural Ena Beçak**, R Oscar Freire 440. **Galeria São Paulo**, R Estados Unidos 1456.

Cinema
Entrance is usually half price on Wed; normal seat price is US$5 in the centre, US$5-6 in R Augusta, Av Paulista and Jardins. Most shopping centres have multiplexes showing the latest blockbuster releases. These are usually in their original language with Portuguese subtitles (*legendas*). Where they are not, they are marked 'DUB' (*dublado*).

There are arts cinemas at the **SESC**s (notably at the **Cine Sesco**, R Augusta 2075, Jardins, T011-3087 0500, www.cinesescsp.org.br, and at **Pompeia** and **Vila Mariana**, www.sesccsp.org.br); at the **Centro Cultural Banco do Brasil** (page 28).

Other arts cinemas are at **Belas Artes** (R da Consalação 2423, T011-3258 4092, www.confrariadecinema.com.br); **Espaço Unibanco** (R Augusta 1470/1475, www.unibancocinemas.com.br); **Museu da Imagem e do Som** (Av Europa 258, T011-2117 4777, www.mis-sp.org.br); **Itaú Cultural**, www.itaucultural.org.br; and **Centro Cultural São Paulo**, www.centrocultural.sp.gov.br (see below).

Classical music, ballet and theatre
Centro Cultural São Paulo, R Vergueiro 1000, T011-3397 4002, www.centrocultural.sp.gov.br. A 50,000-sq-m arts centre with concert halls, where there are regular classical music and ballet recitals – with an orchestral performance most Sun afternoons and a concerto most lunchtimes (in the Sala Adoniran Barbosa), a library with work desks, theatres and exhibition spaces.

Sala São Paulo, see page 30. This magnificent neo-gothic hall with near perfect acoustics is the city's premier classical music venue and is home to Brazil's best orchestra, the Orquestra Sinfônica do Estado de São Paulo (www.osesp.art.br), which is under the helm of French conductor, Yan Pascal Tortelier, former Chief conductor at the BBC Philarmonic and Principal Guest Conductor at the Pittsburgh Symphony Orchestra. The OSESP has been cited as one of 3 up-and-coming ensembles in the ranks of the world's greatest orchestras by the English magazine *Gramophone*. They have a busy schedule of performances with details available on their website and concerts usually every Thu, Fri and Sat.

Teatro Municipal Opera House, see page 30, is used by visiting theatrical and operatic groups, as well as the City Ballet Company and the Municipal Symphony Orchestra, who give regular performances.

There are several other 1st-class theatres: **Aliança Francesa**, R Gen Jardim 182, Vila Buarque, T011-3259 0086; **Itália**, Av Ipiranga 344, T011-3257 9092; **Paiol**, R Amaral Gurgel 164, Santa Cecília, T011-3221 2462; free concerts at **Teatro Popular do Sesi**, Av Paulista 1313, T011-3284 9787, Mon-Sat 1200, under MASP.

Festivals and events

São Paulo *p20, maps p22, p26 and p34*
Throughout the year there are countless anniversaries, religious feasts, fairs and exhibitions. To see what's on, check the local press or the monthly tourist magazines. Fashion week is in the **Bienal Centre** (Bienal do Ibirapuera) in Ibirapuera Park, Parque do Ibirapuera, T011-5576 7600.

25 Jan Foundation of the city.
Feb Carnaval. *Escolas de samba* parade in the Anhembi Sambódromo. During Carnaval most museums and attractions are closed.
Jun Festas Juninas and the **Festa de São Vito**, the patron saint of the Italian immigrants.
Sep Festa da Primavera.
Oct Formula One Grand Prix at Interlagos.
Dec Christmas and New Year festivities.

Shopping

São Paulo *p20, maps p22, p26 and p34*
São Paulo isn't a good place to shop for souvenirs, but it remains Latin America's fashion and accessory capital and, with the possible exception of Melbourne and Sydney (whose industries are far smaller), it is the best location in the southern hemisphere for quality fashion and jewellery.

Books and music

Livrarias Saraiva and **Laselva** are found in various shopping malls and at airports, they sell books in English. **FNAC**, Av Paulista 901 (at Metrô Paraíso) and Praça Omaguás 34, Pinheiros (Metrô Pinheiros), www.fnac.com.br. With a huge choice of DVDs, CDs, books in Portuguese (and English), magazines and newspapers.

Fashion boutiques

São Paulo is one of the newest hot spots on the global fashion circuit and is by far the most influential and diverse fashion city in South America. The designers based here have collections as chic as any in Europe or North America, but at a fraction of the price. Best buys include smart casual day wear, bikinis, shoes, jeans and leather jackets. Havaiana flip flops, made famous by Gisele Bundchen and Fernanda Tavares, are around 10% of the price of Europe. The best areas for fashion shopping are **Jardins** (around R Oscar Freire) and the **Iguatemi shopping centre** (Av Faria Lima). The city's most exclusive shopping emporium is **Daslu**, see page 60.

Adriana Degreas, R Dr Melo Alves 734, Jardins, T011-3064 4300, www.adriana degreas.com.br. Adriana opened her flagship store in Jardins with a zesty collection premiered at Claro Rio Summer fashion show. She now sells at Barneys and Bloomingdales in New York and in Selfridges in London.

Adriana Barra, Alameda Franca 1243, T011-2925 2300, www.adrianabarra.com.br. Showroom in a converted residential house whose façade is entirely covered with vines, bromeliads and ferns. Adriana was already well known for her long dresses and bell-sleeved tunics, made of silk and jersey and printed with designs which take classic belle époque French floral and abstract motifs and reinterpret them in 1970s tropicalia-laced colors and patterns. She now sells homeware – from sofas and scatter cushions to bedspreads, amphorae and notebooks.

Alexandre Herchcovitz, R Haddock Lobo 1151, T011-3063 2889. The most famous Brazilian designer, using brightly coloured materials to create avant garde designs strongly influenced by European trends.

Carina Duek, R Oscar Freire 736, T011-2359 5972, www.carinaduek.com.br. Another rising young star opened this boutique in Oct 2009, designed by Fasano architect Isay Weinfeld. Her simple, figure-hugging light summer dresses and miniskirts – are favourites with 20-something Paulistana socialites.

Fause Haten, Alameda Lorena 1731, Jardins, T011-3081 8685. One of Brazil's most internationally renowned designers who works in plastic, lace, leather, mohair and denim with laminate appliqués, selling through, amongst others, **Giorgio Beverly Hills**.

Forum, R Oscar Freire 916, Jardins T011-3085 6269, www.forum.com.br. A huge white space attended by beautiful shop assistants helping impossibly thin 20-something Brazilians squeeze into tight, but beautifully cut, jeans and other fashion items.

Hotel Lycra, R Oscar Freire 1055, Jardins, T011- 3897 4401, www.hotellycra.com. A favourite shopping spot for the Jardins teenybopper set who park their expensive open-top 18th birthday presents outside and pop in to browse the collection from a rotating selection of young, new Brazilian designers.

Iodice, R Oscar Freire 940, T011-3085 9310, and **Shopping Iguatemi**, T011-3813 2622, www.iodice.com.br. Sophisticated and innovative knitwear designs sold abroad in boutiques like **Barney's NYC**.

Lenny, Shopping Iguatemi, T011-3032 2663, and R Escobar Ortiz 480, Vila Nova Conceicao, T011-3846 6594, www.lenny.com.br. Rio de Janeiro's premier swimwear designer and Brazil's current favourite.

Mario Queiroz, R Alameda Franca 1166, T011-3062 3982, www.marioqueiroz.com.br. Casual and elegant clothes with a strong gay element, for 20-something men.

Ricardo Almeida, Daslu and **Shopping Iguatemi**, T011-3812 6947. One of the few Brazilian designers who styles for men. His clothes are a range of dark suits and slick leather jackets aimed at would-be bit- part actors from *The Matrix*.

Ronaldo Fraga, R Aspicuelta 259, Vila Madalena, T011-3816 2181, www.ronaldo fraga.com. Fraga's adventurous collection combines discipline with daring, retaining a unified style across the sexes yet always surprising and delighting with its off-the- wall creativity.

Rosa Chá, Shopping Higienópolis, Av Higienópolis 418, Metrô Marechal Deodoro, T011-3823 2630, www.rosacha.com.br. One of the world's most sought-after fashion labels for designer swimwear. Beautifully cut bikinis in top-quality materials. Shops in Brazil have cuts exclusive to the country and unavailable in the New York outlet and in London department stores.

UMA, R Girassol 273, T011-3813 5559, www.uma.com.br. Raquel Davidowicz offers rails of sleek contemporary cuts set against low-lit, cool white walls with a Japanese-inspired monochrome minimalism mixed with colourful Brazilian vibrancy.

Victor Hugo, R Oscar Freire 816, T011- 3082 1303, www.victorhugo.com.br. Brazil's most fashionable handbag designer.

Walter Rodrigues, R Natingui 690/696, Vila Madalena, T011-3031 8562. Haute couture for women, renowned for evening gowns that are fluid, sensual and very much inspired by the belle époque.

Zoomp, R Oscar Freire 995, T011-3064 1556, **Shopping Iguatemi**, T011-3032 5372, www.zoomp.com.br. Zoomp have been famous for their figure-hugging jeans for nearly 3 decades and have grown to become a nationwide and now international brand.

Bargain fashion If the upper crust shop and sip coffee in Jardins, the rest of the city buys its wares in the contiguous area of **Bom Retiro**. At first sight the neighbourhood is relentlessly urban: ugly concrete with rows of makeshift houses converted into hundreds of shops selling a bewildering array of clothing. Much of it is trash, and during the week wholesale stores may specify a minimum number of items per buyer. But a few hours browsing will yield clothing bargains to rival those in Bangkok. Many of the outfitters manufacture for the best mid-range labels in São Paulo, including those in **Shopping Ibirapuera** (see below). The best shopping is on and around **R José Paulino** – a street with more than 350 shops. The best day to come is

Sat from 0800, when most items are sold individually.

Shopping 25 de Março, R 25 de Março, www.25demarco.com.br, Metrô São Bento, in the city centre offers a similarly large range of costume jewellery, toys and small decorative items (best on Sat 0800-1430) and the neighbourhood of **Brás** stocks cheaper but lower quality items. For more information see www.omelhordobomretiro.com.br.

Handicrafts

São Paulo has no handicrafts tradition but some items from the rest of Brazil can be bought at **Parque Tte Siqueira Campos/Trianon** on Sun 0900-1700.
Casa dos Amazonas, Av Jurupis 460.
Galeria Arte Brasileira, Av Lorena 2163, T011-3062 9452, www.galeriaartebrasileira.com.br. Stock folk art from the northeast, including the famous clay figurines from Caruaru, Ceará lace, Amazonian hammocks, carved wooden items from all over the country and indigenous Brazilian bead and whicker art.
Sutaco, R Boa Vista 170, Edifício Cidade I, 3rd floor, Centro, T011-3241 7333, www.sutaco.com.br. Handicrafts shop selling and promoting items from the state of São Paulo.

Jewellery

Brazil is one of the world's foremost gemstone producing countries and the largest producer of emeralds. Jewellery is a good buy; though prices are high compared to the rest of Latin America, the stones, setting and craftsmanship of high-end jewellery is on a par with Europe.
H Stern, www.hstern.com.br, with shops all over the city, including R Augusta 2340, R Oscar Freire 652, at Iguatemi, Ibirapuera, Morumbi, Paulista and other shopping centres, at large hotels and at the international airport. Brazil's biggest jewellers, represented in 18 countries. In Brazil they have designs based on Brazilian themes – including Amazonian bead art and Orixa mythology.
Vartanian, NK, R Haddock Lobo 1592, Jardins, T011-3062 2349, www.jackvartanian.com. Jack Vartanian creates fashion jewellery with huge Brazilian emeralds and diamonds set in simple gold and platinum – much beloved of Hollywood red-carpet walkers including Zoe Saldana, Cameron Diaz and Demi Moore. His low-lit Jardins shop showcases jewellery only available only in Brazil.
Antonio Bernardo, R Bela Cintra 2063, Jardins, T011-3083 5622, www.antoniobernardo.com.br. Bernardo is as understated as Vartanian is bling, and offers elegant, contemporary gold and platinum designs and exquisite stones. The designer has branches all over the city and in locations throughout Brazil – full details on website.

Markets

Ceasa flower market, Av Doutor Gastão Vidigal 1946, Jaguaré. Tue and Fri 0700-1200. Should not be missed.
MASP antiques market, takes place below the museum. Sun 1000-1700. Some 50 stalls selling everything from vintage gramophones to ceramics, ornaments and old vinyl.
Mercado Municipal, R da Cantareira 306, Centro, T011-3326 3401, www.mercadomunicipal.com.br, Metrô São Bento. This newly rennovated art deco market was built at the height of the coffee boom and is illuminated by beautiful stained-glass panels by Conrado Sorgenicht Filho showing workers tilling the soil. It's worth coming here just to browse aisles bursting with produce – *açai* from the Amazon, hunks of *bacalhau* from the North Sea, mozzarella from Minas, sides of beef from the Pantanal and 1000 other foodstuffs. The upper gallery has half a dozen restaurants offering dishes of the day and a vantage point over the frenetic buying and selling below.

Oriental Fair, Praça de Liberdade. Sun 1000-1900. Good for Japanese snacks, plants and some handicrafts, very picturesque, with remedies on sale, tightrope walking, gypsy fortune tellers, etc.

Praça Benedito Calixto, Pinheiros, the best bric-a-brac market in São Paulo takes place here, www.pracabeneditocalixto.com.br. Sat 0900-1900. Live *choro* and samba 1430- 1830, Metrô Pinheiros. Stalls in the square and in the surrounding streets sell arts, crafts, CDs, T-shirts and second-hand goods. There is live *choro* and *samba* music and good food and there are many stylish arts and crafts and fashion shops, restaurants and cafés around the square.

Av **Lorena**, which is one of the upmarket shopping streets off R Augusta in Jardins, has an open-air market on Sun selling fruits and juices. There is a flea market on Sun in **Praça Don Orione** (main square of the Bixiga district).

Shopping malls and department stores

For more information on shopping malls, see www.shoppingsdesaopaulo.com.br.
Daslu, Av Chedid Jafat 131, T011-3841 3000, www.daslu.com.br. This temple to snobbery is worth visiting if only for anthropological reasons. It is the fashion store of choice for South America's high society and it's not uncommon for customers to fly in from Argentina or Mato Grosso on private planes and spend up to US$50,000 in a single shopping spree. Collections include that of Daslu itself, alongside up-and-coming Brazilian names like **Juliana Jabour**, **Cris Barros**, www.crisbarros.com.br, and **Raia de Goeye**, www.raiadegoeye.com.br, and big- name international designers. These sit along- side boutiques selling everything from high- class wines to beautiful coffee-table books.
Shopping Cidade Jardim, Av Magalhães de Castro 12000, T011-3552 1000, www.cidadejardimshopping.com.br, CPTM Hebraica- Rebouças (and then 5-10 mins by taxi). The city's newest upmarket mall is a vast, neoclassical edifice with a lush tropical garden in its interior and towering skyscraper apartment blocks above. It is filled with Brazilian names like **Carlos Miele** and **Osklen**, whose casual beach and adventure clothes look like Ralph Lauren gone tropical and are aimed at a similar yacht-and-boardwalk crowd. International names include **Hermes** and there is a branch of **Daslu**, which, unlike their store across the river, has changing rooms. There's a spa at the mall, too, as well as a branch of the informal Italian bistro **Nono Ruggero** and an outpost of the popular upmarket Brazilian-Japanese chain **Kosushi**. The shopping mall has a cinema.
Shopping D, Av Cruzeiro do Sul 1100, Canindé, T011-3311 9333. Some 320 shops with many clothes in the middle to low price ranges. On the edge of the city near the river And immediately opposite the Terminal Tietê *rodoviária*. With a cinema.
Shopping Ibirapuera, Av Ibirapuera 3103, www.ibirapuera.com.br, Metrô Ana Rosa and bus 695V (Terminal Capelinha). A broad selection of mid-range Brazilian labels and general shops including toy and book shops.
Shopping Iguatemi, Av Brigadeiro Faria Lima 2232, www.iguatemisaopaulo.com.br. Another top-end shopping mall just south of Jardins with a healthy representation of most of Brazil's foremost labels.

▲ Activities and tours

São Paulo *p20, maps p22, p26 and p34*
Football
The most popular local teams are Corinthians, Palmeiras and São Paulo who generally play in the Morumbi and Pacaembu stadiums.

Tour operators
São Paulo has several large agencies offering tours around the country.
Ambiental Viagens e Expedições, www.ambiental.tur.br. Good for trips to less well known places throughout the country

like Jalapão. English and Spanish spoken, helpful.

Matueté, R Tapinás 22, Itaim, T011- 3071 4515, www.matuete.com. Luxury breaks throughout Brazil and city tours, including personal shopping. Ask for Camilla. English spoken.

Trip on Jeep, R Arizona 623, Brooklin, T011-5543 5281, www.triponjeep.com. Wonderful day or weekend trips away from the heat and the dust of São Paulo city to the lush, green bird and wildlife filled forests nearby, to the caves in PETAR and destinations throughout the state of São Paulo. The company run tours in comfortable Land Rovers and these are conducted by English-speaking zoologists and botanists. The Parelheiros trip includes organic lunch at the Centro Paulus – a delightful haven in secondary forest. Highly recommended.

Tropico Turismo, T011-4025 9281, www.tropico.tur.br. Adventure day trips around São Paulo including rappelling, zip-lines and canopy walking, whitewater rafting and hikes. English spoken. Well organized.

Transport

São Paulo *p20, maps p22, p26 and p34*
Air
See also Getting there, page 6.
Guarulhos international airport (**Cumbica**) operates services to all parts of the world and much of Brazil. The cheapest internal flights are with **TAM**, www.tam.com.br, **GOL**, www.voegol.com.br, **Azul**, www.voeazul.com.br (who fly from Campinas, page 6), and **Avianca**, www.avianca.com.br. To get to the airport, **Emtu** buses run every 30 mins from Praça da República 343 (northwest side, corner of R Arouche), 0530-2300, and from Rodoviária Tietê, US$6.50, 30-45 mins. Buses also run from Bresser bus station and there are buses from Jabaquara bus terminal, without luggage space, usually crowded. Taxi fares from the city to the airport are US$60-80. Rush-hour traffic can easily turn this 30-min journey into an hour or even longer. Be sure to arrive with plenty of time for checking in as long queues form for immigration and customs: passenger numbers have doubled at Cumbica over the past decade and the airport is becoming increasingly crowded.

Congonhas domestic airport is used for flights within Brazil, including the shuttle flight with **Rio de Janeiro** (Santos Dumont airport, US$100-150 single, depending on availability). The shuttle services operate every 30 mins throughout the day from 0630-2230. Sit on the left-hand side for views to Rio de Janeiro, the other side coming back, book flights in advance. To get to Congonhas airport, take an **Emtu** bus the centre or a taxi, US$20.

Bus
There are 4 bus terminals: **Tietê**, **Barra Funda**, **Bresser** and **Jabaquara**. All are connected to the metrô system. To search for bus routes and times, see www.passagem-em-domicilio.com.br/terminal-tiete.asp. The site gives times and routes and redirects to the bus company website for the service, through which it is possible to buy tickets.

Rodoviária Tietê This is the main bus station and has a convenient metrô station. Unfortunately the only way to the platforms is by stairs which makes it very difficult for people with heavy luggage and almost impossible for those in a wheelchair. Tietê handles buses to the interior of São Paulo state, to all state capitals and international destinations. To **Rio**, 6 hrs, every 30 mins, US$12.50 (*leito* US$35), special section for this route in the *rodoviária*, request the coastal route via Santos (*via litoral*) unless you wish to go the direct route. To **Florianópolis**, 11 hrs, US$120 (*leito* US$150). To **Porto Alegre**, 18 hrs, US$160 (*leito* US$190). To **Curitiba**, 6 hrs, US$80. To **Salvador**, 30 hrs, US$130 (*leito* US$170). To **Recife**, 40 hrs, US$160-180.

To **Campo Grande**, 14 hrs, US$80. To **Cuiabá**, 24 hrs, US$110. To **Porto Velho**, 60 hrs (or more), US$160. To **Brasília**, 16 hrs, US$100 (*leito* US$120). To **Foz do Iguaçu**, 16 hrs, US$90. To **São Sebastião**, 4 hrs, US$30 (ask for 'via Bertioga' if you want to go by the coast road, a beautiful journey but few buses take this route as it is longer).

International connections Buses to Uruguay include: **Montevideo**, via Porto Alegre, cold a/c at night, plenty of meal stops, bus stops for border formalities, passengers disembark only to collect passport and tourist card on the Uruguayan side. Buses to Paraguay include: **Asunción** (1044 km), 18 hrs with **Pluma**, US$180 (*leito* US$200), **Brújula** (US$170) or **RYSA** (US$200), all stop at **Ciudad del Este** (US$100, US$130 and US$150 respectively, Pluma *leito* US$180). Cometa del Amambay runs to **Pedro Juan Caballero** and **Concepción**. To **Buenos Aires** (Argentina), **Pluma**, 36 hrs, US$240. To **Santiago** (Chile), (**Pluma** or **Chilebus**, 56 hrs, US$240 (**Chilebus**, poor meals, but otherwise good, beware of overbooking).

Barra Funda (Metrô Barra Funda), to cities in southern **São Paulo state** and many destinations in Paraná, including **Foz do Iguaçu** (check for special prices on buses to **Ciudad del Este**, which can be cheaper than buses to Foz). Buses run to **Cananéia** daily at 0900 and 1430, 4 hrs. Alternatively go via **Registro** (buses hourly), from where there are 7 buses daily to Cananéia and regular connections to **Curitiba**.

Bresser (Metrô Bresser), for **Cometa** (T011-6967 7255) or **Transul** (T011-6693 8061) serving destinations in Minas Gerais. **Belo Horizonte**, 10 hrs, US$80, 11 a day (*leito* US$100), 9 a day with **Gontijo**. **Translavras** and **Util** also operate out of this station. Prices are given under destinations. See www.passagem-em-domicilio.com.br for more information including bus times and the latest prices.

Jabaquara (at the southern end of the metrô line), is used by buses to **Santos**, US$5, every 15 mins, taking about 50 mins, last bus at 0100. Also serves destinations on the southern coast of São Paulo state.

Car hire
The major names all serve São Paulo and have offices at the airports.

CPTM (urban light railway)
→ *See map, p8*

Ticket prices on the CPTM are the same as the metrô (see below and box, above).
Linha 7 Rubi (ruby) runs from Jundiaí, a satellite commuter town, to the Estação da Luz via Barra Funda and the Palmeiras football stadium.
Linha 8 Diamante (diamond) runs from Amador Bueno to the Estação Júlio Prestes railway station in Luz, near the Pinacoteca and next to the Estação da Luz.
Linha 9 Esmeralda (emerald) runs between the suburb of Osasco and the suburb of Grajaú in the far south. This is the most useful line for tourists as it runs along the Pinheiros river, stopping at the Cidade Universitária (for Butantã), Hebraica-Rebouças (for shopping Eldorado and the Azul bus to Campinas airport, see page 7), Cidade Jardim (for Shopping Cidade Jardim and Daslu malls, see page 60), Vila Olímpia (close to one of the nightlife centres) and Berrini (in the new business district). The line connects with the metrô at the new Pinheiros metrô station on the Linha Amarela.
Linha 10 Turquesa (turquoise) runs from Rio Grande da Serra in the Serra do Mar mountains (from where there are onward trains to Paranapiacaba, see page 42) to the Estação da Luz.
Linha 11 Coral (coral) runs from the Estudantes suburb to the Estação da Luz.
Linha 12 Safira (sapphire) runs from Calmon Viana suburb to Brás.

O Bilhete Único

This electronic ticket is similar to a London Oyster card – integrating bus, metro and light railway in a single, rechargeable plastic swipe card. US$2 serves for one metro or CPTM journey and three bus journeys within the space of three hours. Swipe cards can be bought at metro stations. The initial minimum charge is US$10.

Metrô → *See map, p8*

Directions are indicated by the name of the terminus station. Network maps are displayed only in the upper concourses of the metrô stations; there are none on the platforms. Many of the maps on the internet are confusing as they incorporate the CPTM overground train routes, also with colour codes. Journeys can get extremely crowded at peak times (0700-1000, 1630-1900). Services are also plagued by unannounced and unexplained stops and cancellations. Fares are at a flat rate of US$1.50, or R$20 for a book of 10 tickets. A combined bus and metrô ticket costs R$2.20; useful for getting to Congonhas airport; see also box, page 63.

Linha 1 Azul (blue), runs from Tucuruvi in the north to the Rodoviária Jabaraquara in the south and passing through Luz, the centre and Liberdade.

Linha 2 Verde (green) runs from Vila Madalena to Vila Prudente, via Av Paulista and the MASP art gallery.

Linha 3 Vermelha (red) runs from the Palmeiras football stadium in Barra Funda to the Corinthians football stadium in Itaquera, via the city centre.

Linha 4 Amarela (yellow) running between between Morumbi football stadium (which will be used for the World Cup) and Luz, via USP University at Butantã, Oscar Freire in Jardins and Av Paulista; due to open in 2011.

Linha 5 Lilás (lilac) running in São Paulo's far southwest, between Capão Redondo favela and Adolfo Pinheiro, with an extension to Chacara Klabin on the 2 Verde line with stations opening between 2011 and 2014.

Taxi

Taxis display cards of actual tariffs in the window (starting price US$4). There are ordinary taxis, which are hailed on the street, or at taxi stations such as Praça da República, radio taxis and deluxe taxis. For **Radio Taxis**, which are more expensive but involve fewer hassles, **Central Radio Táxi**, T011-6914 6630; **São Paulo Rádio Táxi**, T011-5583 2000; **Fácil**, T011-6258 5947; **Aero Táxi**, T011-6461 4090; or look in the phone book; calls are not accepted from public phones.

Trains

From **Estação da Luz** and **Estação Júlio Prestes** (Metrô Luz).

Directory

São Paulo *p20, maps p22, p26 and p34*
Banks Banking hours are generally 1000-1600, although times differ for foreign exchange. For ATMS, the best bank to use is **Bradesco**, www.bradesco.com.br or **HSBC**, www.hsbc.com.br, which have branches on every other street corner and ATMs in the airport and all the major shopping malls. Be wary when using ATMs and never use street machines after dark. Most ATMs do not function between 2200 and 0600. **Banco do Brasil** will change cash and TCs and will advance cash against Visa. All transactions are done in the foreign exchange department of any main branch (eg Av São João 32, Centro), but queues are long and commission very high. **Embassies and consulates Argentina**, Av Paulista 2313, T011-3897 9522 (0900-1300), argentina.visahq.com, very easy to get a visa here. **Australia**, 9th floor, Unit 92

Edifício Trianon Corporate, Alamenda Santos 700, Jardins, T011-2112 6200, www.brazil.embassy.gov.au. **Bolivia**, Av Paulista 1439, T011-3289 0443, www.cgb.org.br. **Canada**, Av das Nações Unidas 12901, 16 andar, T011-5509 4343, www.canadainternational.gc.ca. **France**, Av Paulista 1842, 14th floor, T011-3371 5400, saopaulo.ambafrance-br.org. **Germany**, Av Brigadeiro Faria Lima 2092, T011-3097 6644, www.brasil.diplo.de. **Ireland**, Honorary Consul, Al Joaquim Eugenio de Lima 447, T011 3147 7788, www.dfa.ie. **Israel**, Av Brig Faria Lima 1713, T011-3031 6594. **New Zealand**, Av Campinas 579, T011-3148 0489. **Paraguay**, R Bandeira Paulista 600, 15th floor, T011-3167 6397, www.paraguay sp.com.br. **Peru**, R Guadelupe 28, T011-3063 5152, www.consuladopersp.com.br. **South Africa**, Av Paulista 1754, T011-3253 8806. **UK**, R Ferreira de Araujo 74, 2 Andar Pinheiros, T011-3094 2700, ukinbrazil.fco.gov.uk **Uruguay**, R Estados Unidos 1284, T011-2879 6600, www.emburuguai.org.br). **US**, R Henri Dunant 500, Chácara Santo Antônio, T011-5186 7000, www.embaixada-americana.org.br **Venezuela**, R General Fonseca Teles, 564, T011-3887 2535. **Immigration Federal Police**, R. Hugo D'Antola 95, Lapa de Baixo, T011-3538 5000, www.dpf.gov.br. For visa extensions. Allow all day and expect little English (1000-1600). **Internet** Too ubiquitous to list – look for any LAN house sign. **Language courses** The official

Universidade de São Paulo (USP) is situated in the Cidade Universitária (buses from main bus station), beyond Pinheiros. They have courses available to foreigners, including a popular Portuguese course. Registry is through the **Comissão de Cooperação Internacional**, R do Anfiteatro 181, Bloco das Colméias 05508, Cidade Universitária, São Paulo. Other universities include the **Pontifical Catholic University (PUC)**, and the **Mackenzie University**. Both these are more central than the USP, Mackenzie in Higienopolis, just west of the centre, and PUC in Perdizes. Take a taxi to either. Both have noticeboards where you can leave a request for Portuguese teachers or language exchange, which is easy to arrange for free. Any of the *gringo* pubs are good places to organize similar exchanges. **Laundry Chuá Self Service**, R Augusta 728, limited self-service, not cheap. **Di-Lelles**, R Atenas 409, pricey. **Medical services Hospital das Clínicas**, Av Dr Enéias de Carvalho Aguiar 255, Jardins, T011-3069 6000. **Hospital Samaritano**, R Cons Brotero 1468, Higenópolis, T011-3824 0022. Recommended. Both have *pronto-socorro* (emergency services). Contact your consulate for names of doctors and dentists who speak your language. **Emergency and ambulance**: T192. **Fire**: T193. **Post office Correio Central**, Correios – yellow and blue signs – eg Praça do Correio, corner of Av São João and Prestes Máia, T011-3831 5222.

The coast of São Paulo

São Paulo's coast is packed at the weekend (when the city dwellers leave for the beach) and deserted during the week. There are many beautiful beaches to choose from: some backed by rainforest-covered mountains and all washed by a bottle-green warm Atlantic. The best are along the northernmost part of the state coast, the Litoral Norte, around Ubatuba, and along the Litoral Sul near Cananéia. There are beautiful islands too including Brazil's largest, Ilhabela, and her wildest, Ilha do Cardoso. The dividing point between the Litoral Norte and Litoral Sul is the historic city of Santos; made most famous by Pelé (there's a museum devoted to him), and dotted with a few interesting buildings and museums in a spruced-up, attractive colonial city centre. ›› *For listings, see pages 78-85.*

Santos and São Vicente → *For listings, see pages 78-85. Phone code: 013. Population: 418,000.*

The Portuguese knew how to choose a location for a new settlement. **Santos** stands on an island in a bay surrounded by towering mountains and extensive areas of lowland mangrove forest – a setting equally as beautiful as that of Salvador or Rio. When it was dominated by colonial houses, churches and clean white-sand beaches Santos itself must have been one of Brazil's most enchanting cities. But in the 20th century an evil reputation for yellow fever and industrial pollution from nearby Cubatão left the city to decay and it lost much of its architecture along with its charm. Contemporary Santos, however, is getting its act together. The old colonial centre has been tidied up and Scottish trams ferry tourists past the city's sights. These include a series of colonial churches and the Bolsa do Café – a superb little museum whose café-restaurant serves the most delicious espresso in Brazil. Santos is also Pelé's home and the city he played for almost all his career. Santos FC has a museum devoted to the club and to Pelé and it is easy to attend a game.

On the mainland, **São Vicente** is, to all intents and purposes, a suburb of Santos, having been absorbed into the conurbation. It was the first town founded in Brazil, in 1532, but nowadays it is scruffy and with very few sights of interest but for the rather dilapidated colonial church, the Matriz São Vicente Mártir (1542, rebuilt in 1757) in the Praça do Mercado. The Litoral Sul (see page 74) begins after São Vicente.

Ins and outs

Getting there Santos is served by regular buses from São Paulo as well as towns along the Litoral Norte and Litoral Sul, such as Curitibia, Rio de Janeiro and Florianópolis. Buses arrive at the **rodoviária** ① *Praça dos Andradas 45, T013-3219 2194*, close to the colonial centre. Those from São Paulo also stop at Ponta da Praia and José Menino, which are nearer to the main hotel district in Gonzaga. A taxi to Gonzaga from the bus station costs about US$7; all taxis have meters.

Getting around The best way to get around the centre of Santos is by the newly restored Victorian trams, which leave on guided tours (Tue-Sun 1100-1700) from in front of the Prefeitura Municipal on Praça Visconde de Maúa. The tram passes most of the interesting sights, including the *azulejo*-covered houses on Rua do Comércio, the Bolsa do Café and some of the oldest churches. Local buses run from the colonial centre and *rodoviária* to the seafront – look for Gonzaga or Praia on their destination plaque. Bus fares within Santos are US$0.60; to São Vicente US$0.90.

Orientation The centre of the city is on the north side of the island. Due south, on the Baía de Santos, is **Gonzaga**, São Paulo's favourite beach resort where much of the city's entertainment takes place. Between these two areas, the eastern end of the island curves round within the Santos Channel. At the eastern tip, a ferry crosses the estuary to give access to the busy beaches of Guarujá and Praia Grande. The city has impressive modern buildings, wide, tree-lined avenues, and wealthy suburbs.

Tourist information There are SETUR offices at the *rodoviária*, at Praía do Gonzaga on the seafront (in a disused tram – very helpful, lots of leaflets), and next to the British railway

Santos

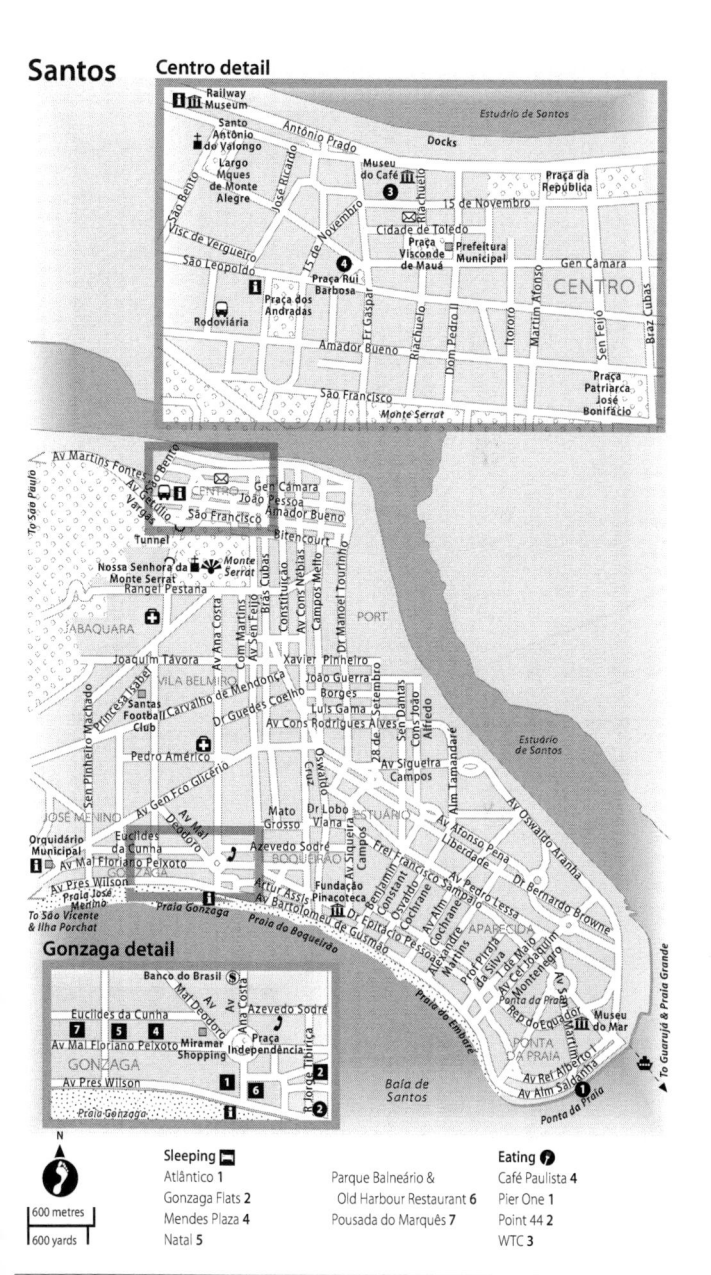

Centro detail

Gonzaga detail

N
600 metres
600 yards

Sleeping
Atlântico **1**
Gonzaga Flats **2**
Mendes Plaza **4**
Natal **5**
Parque Balneário &
 Old Harbour Restaurant **6**
Pousada do Marquês **7**

Eating
Café Paulista **4**
Pier One **1**
Point 44 **2**
WTC **3**

São Paulo Santos & São Vicente • 67

station – Estação do Valongo, Largo Marquês de Monte Alegre s/n, T013-3201 8000 www.santos.sp.gov.br, Monday-Friday 1000-1600, Saturday 1000-1400. Although poverty is apparent, the city is generally safe. However, it is wise to exercise caution at night and near the port.

Background

Santos is one of Brazil's oldest cities and has long been its most important port. The coast around the city is broken by sambaqui shell mounds that show the area has been inhabited by humans since at least 5000 BC. When the Portuguese arrived, the Tupinikin people dominated the region. However, the first settlements at neighbouring São Vicente (1532) were constantly under attack by the Tamoio who were allies of the French. The French were defeated at Rio in 1560 and the Tamoio massacred soon after.

By the 1580s Santos was a burgeoning port with some 400 houses. The first export was sugar, grown as cane at the foot of the mountains and on the plateau. By the late 19th century this had been replaced by coffee, which rapidly became Brazil's main source of income. The city was connected to São Paulo and the coffee region by the British under the guidance of Barão Visconde de Mauá, and the city grew wealthy. The seafront was lined with opulent coffee mansions and the centre was home to Brazil's most important stock exchange, the Bolsa do Café.

In the 1980s, the hinterland between the sea and mountains became the site of one of South America's most unpleasant industrial zones. The petrochemical plants of Cubatão were so notorious that they were referred to in the press as the 'The Valley of Death'. Santos and around was said to be the most contaminated corner of the planet, with so much toxic waste undermining the hills that the whole lot threatened to slip down into the sea. In the late 1980s, a spate of mutant births in Cubatão eventually prompted a clean-up operation, which is said to have been largely successful.

Sights

The heart of the colonial centre is **Praça Mauá**. The surrounding streets are very lively in the daytime, with plenty of cheap shops and restaurants. The most interesting buildings are to be found here and all can be visited by tram. The most impressive is the **Museu do Café** ① *R 15 de Novembro 95, T013-3219 5585, www.museudocafe.com.br, Tue-Sat 0900-1700, Sun 1000-1700, US$2*, housed in the old Bolsa Oficial de Café. Its plain exterior hides a grand marble-floored art deco stock exchange and museum, with a café serving some of the best coffee and cakes in South America. The building was once open only to wealthy (and exclusively male) coffee barons who haggled beneath a magnificent stained-glass skylight, depicting a bare-breasted Brazil – the *Mãe Douro* – crowned with a star in a tropical landscape populated with tropical animals and perplexed indigenous Brazilians. The skylight and the beautiful neo-Renaissance painting of Santos that decorates the walls of the exchange is by Brazil's most respected 19th-century artist, Benedito Calixto, who was born in Santos. One of the few remaining coffee baron mansions, the **Fundação Pinacoteca** ① *Av Bartolomeu de Gusmão 15, T013-3288 2260, www.pinacoteca.unisanta.br, Tue-Sun 1400-1900, free*, on the seafront, is now a gallery housing some of his paintings, most of them landscapes, which give some idea of the city's original beauty.

Santos has a few interesting and ancient colonial churches. Only the **Santuário Santo Antônio do Valongo** ① *Marquez de Monte Alegre s/n, Tue-Sun 0800-1700, guided tours*

> ### Great Burnt Island
>
> Off the shore of Brazil, almost due south of the heart of São Paulo, is Allha de Queimada Grande – Great Burnt Island – untouched by human developers and feared by locals. And for good reason – zoologists estimate that there are between one and five snakes per square metre on the island; a figure which might be tolerable were they harmless garter snakes. However, Queimada Grande's snakes are a unique species of pit viper, the golden lancehead. The lancehead genus of snakes is responsible for 90% of Brazilian snakebite-related fatalities. Golden lanceheads on Queimada Grande grow to well over half a metre long, and they possess a powerful fast-acting poison that melts the flesh around their bites. This place is so dangerous that a permit is required to visit.

most days after 1000, in Portuguese only, is regularly open to the public. Its twee mock-baroque interior is from the 1930s, but the far more impressive original 17th-century altarpiece sits in the Franciscan chapel to the left of the main entrance. The statue of Christ is particularly fine. Next door to the church is the British-built terminus of the now defunct Santos–São Paulo railway, which serves as a small museum. The tourist office sits above it.

On Avenida Ana Costa there is an interesting monument to commemorate the brothers Andradas, who took a leading part in the movement for Independence. There are other monuments on Praça Rui Barbosa to Bartolomeu de Gusmão, who has a claim to the world's first historically recorded airborne ascent in 1709; in the Praça da República to Brás Cubas, who founded the city in 1534; and in the Praça José Bonifácio to the soldiers of Santos who died in the Revolution of 1932.

Brazil's iconic football hero, Pelé, played for Santos for almost all his professional life, signing when he was in his teens. **Santos Football Club** ⓘ *R Princesa Isabel 77, Vila Belmiro, T013-3257 4000, http://santos.globo.com, Mon 1300-1900, Tue-Sun 0900-1900, US$3, for tours of the grounds call T013-3225 7989*, has an excellent museum, the Memorial das Conquistas, which showcases not only Pelé (with his kit, boots and other assorted personal items on display), but the history of the club. Its collection of gold and silver includes several international championship trophies. Pelé still lives in the city and can sometimes be seen at matches. It is possible to see Santos play; details available on their website.

Monte Serrat, just south of the city centre, has at its summit a semaphore station and look-out post which reports the arrival of all ships in Santos harbour. There is also an old church, **Nossa Senhora da Monte Serrat**, where the patron, Our Lady of Montserrat, is said to have performed many miracles.

The top can be reached on foot or by **funicular**, which leaves every 30 minutes (US$6). Seven shrines have been built on the way up and annual pilgrimages are made by the local people. There are fine views.

In the western district of José Menino is the **Orquidário Municipal** ⓘ *Praça Washington, orchid garden Tue-Sun 0900-1700, bird enclosure 0800-1100, 1400-1700, US$0.50*. The flowers bloom from October to February and there is an orchid show in November. Visitors can wander among giant subtropical and tropical trees, amazing orchids and, when the aviary is open, meet macaws, toucans and parrots. The open-air cage contains hummingbirds of 20 different species and the park is a sanctuary for other birds.

Beaches

Santo has 8 km of beaches stretching round the Baía de Santos to those of São Vicente at the western end. From east to west they are **Ponta da Praia**, below the sea wall and on the estuary, no good for bathing, but fine for watching the movements of the ships. Next are **Aparecida**, **Embaré**, **Boqueirão**, **Gonzaga** and **José Menino** (the original seaside resort for the merchants of Santos). São Vicente's beaches of **Itararé** and **Ilha Porchat** are on the island, while **Gonzaguinha** is on the mainland. The last beach is **Itaquitanduva**, which is in a military area but may be visited with authorization. In all cases, check the cleanliness of the water before venturing in (a red flag means it is too polluted for bathing).

Excursions from Santos

The small island of **Ilha Porchat** is reached by a bridge at the far end of Santos/São Vicente bay. It has beautiful views over rocky precipices, of the high seas on one side and of the city and bay on the other. At the summit is **Terraço Chopp** ① *Av Ary Barroso 274*, a restaurant with live music most evenings and great views. On summer evenings the queues can be up to four hours, but in winter, even if it may be a little chilly at night, you won't have to wait.

Litoral Norte → *For listings, see pages 78-85.*

The resorts immediately north of Santos – Guarujá, Praia Grande and Bertioga – are built-up and none too clean. It becomes more beautiful at Camburi, the southernmost beach of São Sebastião province, named after the historical town that sits in front of Ilhabela, an island fringed with glorious beaches. Further north, Ubatuba, borders the state of Rio de Janeiro and has dozens of beautiful stretches of golden sand backed by forest-covered mountains.

Camburi, Camburizinho and Maresias → *Phone code: 012.*

Beyond Boracéia are a number of beaches, including Barra do Una, Praia da Baleia and **Camburi**. The latter is the first beach in São Sebastião province and is surrounded by the *Mata Atlântica* forest. It has a long stretch of sand with some surf, many *pousadas* and two of the best restaurants in São Paulo state. The best place for swimming is at **Camburizinho** (though you should avoid swimming in the river which is not clean). You can walk on the Estrada do Piavu into the *Mata Atlântica* to see vegetation and wildlife; bathing in the streams is permitted, but use of shampoo and other chemicals is forbidden. About 5 km from Camburi is **Praia Brava**, 45 minutes' walk through the forest. The surf here is very heavy, hence the name. Camping is possible.

The road continues from Camburi, past beaches such as **Boiçucanga** (family-orientated with many *pousadas*) to **Maresias**, which is beloved of well-to-do Paulistas who come here mostly to surf. It has some chic *pousadas* and restaurants and tends to be younger and less family orientated than Camburi.

São Sebastião → *Phone code: 012. Population: 59,000.*

From Maresias it is 21 km to São Sebastião, which was once as attractive as Paraty and still retains a pretty colonial centre. Ferries leave from here for the 15-minute crossing to **Ilhabela** (see page 71), the largest offshore island in Brazil, which is shrouded in forest on its ocean side and fringed with some of São Paulo's best beaches.

The city was founded at the time when Brazil's rainforest stretched all the way from the coast to the Pantanal, and all the land north to Rio de Janeiro was ruled by the indigenous Tamoio and their French allies. The settlement was initially created as an outpost of the indigenous slave trade and a port from which to dispatch armies to fight the French and claim Rio for the Portuguese crown. After this was achieved and the Tamoio had been massacred, São Sebastião grew to become one of Brazil's first sugar-exporting ports and the hinterland was covered in vast fields of cane tilled by the enslaved indigenous Brazilians. When the number of local slaves became depleted by the lash and disease, the city became one of the first ports of the African slave trade.

Ins and outs São Sebastião is served by regular buses from Ubatuba and Santos and is also connected to São Paulo. Ferries (for cars as well as passengers), US$2, from Ilhabela run 24 hours a day (see page 84) and take 15 minutes. The **tourist office** ① *R Sebastião Silvestre Neves 214, T012-3892 5323, www.saosebastiao.sp.gov.br, daily 1000-1700*, lies on the waterfront one block towards the sea from Praça Major João Fernandes. Staff are very helpful and can provide maps and information on ferries to Ilhabela and beaches in the entire São Sebatstião province. The city is far cheaper for accommodation than Ilhabela.

Sights São Sebastião's remaining colonial streets are in the few blocks between the shoreline and the Praça Major João Fernandes, which is dominated by the **Igreja Matriz** ① *daily 0900-1800*. Although this retains remnants of its original 17th-century design, this is predominantly a 19th-century reconstruction devoid of much of its original church art. However, the newly refurbished **Museu de Arte Sacra** ① *1 block south of the praça, R Sebastião Neves 90, T012-3892 4286, daily 1300-1700, free*, in the 17th-century chapel of São Gonçalo, preserves a number of 16th-century statues found in cavities in the wall of the Igreja Matriz during its restoration in 2003.

The city has a few sleepy streets of Portuguese houses, fanning out from the square, and a handful of civic buildings worth a quick look before the ferry leaves for Ilhabela. The most impressive is the **Casa Esperança** ① *Av Altino Arantes 154, not open to the public although they often let visitors in on request*, on the waterfront. It was built from stone and wattle and daub glued together with whale oil, and then whitewashed with lime from thousands of crushed shells collected on the beaches of Ilhabela. The interior has some peeling 17th-century ceiling paintings.

Ilhabela (Ilha de São Sebastião)
→ *Phone code: 012. Population: 21,000 (100,000 high season).*

Ilhabela is Brazil's largest oceanic island and one of its prettiest. It is wild enough to be home to ocelots, and the lush forests on its ocean side (80% of which are protected by a state park) drip with waterfalls and are fringed with glorious beaches. Its centre is crowned with craggy peaks, often obscured by mist: **Morro de São Sebastião** (1379 m), **Morro do Papagaio** (1309 m), **Ramalho** (1285 m) and **Pico Baepi** (1025 m). Rainfall on the island is heavy, about 3000 mm a year, and there are many small biting flies known locally as *borrachudos*.

The island is considered the 'Capital da Vela' (capital of sailing) because its 150 km of coastline offers all types of conditions. The sheltered waters of the strait are where many sailors learn their skills and the bays around the coast provide safe anchorages. There are, however, numerous tales of shipwrecks because of the unpredictable winds, sudden mists and strange forces playing havoc with compasses, but these provide plenty of adventure for divers. There are over 30 wrecks that can be dived, the most notable being the *Príncipe de Asturias*, a transatlantic liner that went down off the Ponta de Pirabura in 1916.

Ins and outs There are good transport connections with the mainland. **Litorânea** buses from São Paulo connect with a service right through to Ilhabela town. Ferries run day and night and leave regularly from the São Sebastião waterfront, taking about 20 minutes; free for pedestrians, cars US$1 weekdays, US$10 at weekends. It is very difficult to find space for a car on the ferry during summer weekends. A bus meets the ferry and runs to Ilhabela town and along the west coast. Try to visit during the week when the island feels deserted, and avoid high season (December to February) at all costs. Hotels and *pousadas* are expensive; many people choose to stay in São Sebastião instead. For information contact the **Secretaria de Turismo** ① *Praça Ver, José Leite dos Passos 14, Barra Velha, T012-3895 7220, www.ilhabela.sp.gov.br.* ▸▸ *See Transport, page 84.*

Sights Most of the island's residents live on the sheltered shore facing the mainland, along which are a number of upmarket *pousadas*. Swimming is not recommended on this side of the island within 4 km of São Sebastião because of pollution. Watch out for oil, sandflies and jellyfish on the sand and in the water.

About 20 minutes north of the ferry terminal is the main population centre, **Vila Ilhabela**. The village has some pretty colonial buildings and the parish church, **Nossa Senhora da Ajuda e Bom Sucesso**, dates from the 17th century and has been restored. There are restaurants, cafés and shops. Four kilometres north of Ilhabela, **Pedras do Sino** (Bell Rocks) are curious seashore boulders which, when struck with a piece of iron or stone, emit a loud bell-like note. There is a beach here and a campsite nearby.

From Vila Ilhabela, the road hugs the coast, sometimes high above the sea, towards the south of the island. An old *fazenda*, **Engenho d'Água**, a few kilometres from town in a grand 18th-century mansion (not open to the public), gives its name to one of the busiest beaches. About 10 km further, you can visit the old **Feiticeira** plantation. It has underground dungeons, and can be reached by bus, taxi, or horse and buggy. A trail leads down from the plantation to the beautiful beach of the same name.

On the south coast is the fishing village of **Bonete**, which has 500 m of beach and can be reached either by boat (1½ hours), or by driving to Borrifos at the end of the road, then walking along a a rainforest-covered trail for three hours – a beautiful walk.

Much of the Atlantic side of the island is protected by the **Parque Estadual de Ilhabela**. There is a dirt road across to the east of the island, but it requires a 4WD. A few kilometres along this road is a turning to the terraced waterfall of **Cachoeira da Toca** (US$4). Set in dense jungle close to the foot of the Baepi peak, the cool freshwater pools are good for bathing and attract lots of butterflies. The locals claim that there are more than 300 waterfalls on the island, but only a few of them can be reached on foot; those that can are worth the effort. There is a 50-km return trek from Vila Ilhabela over the hump of the island down towards the Atlantic. The route follows part of the old slave trail and requires a local guide as it negotiates dense tropical forest. It takes at least two days.

Some of the island's best beaches are on the Atlantic side of the island and can only be reached by boat. **Praia dos Castelhanos** is recommended. At the cove of **Saco do Sombrio** English, Dutch and French pirates sheltered in the 16th and 17th centuries.

Needless to say, this has led to legends of hidden treasure, but the most potent story about the place is that of the Englishman, Thomas Cavendish. In 1592 he sacked Santos and set it on fire. He then sailed to Saco do Sombrio where his crew mutinied, hanged Cavendish, sank their boats and settled on the island.

Ubatuba → *For listings, see pages 78-85. Phone code: 012. Population: 67,000.*

This is one of the most beautiful stretches of the São Paulo coast and has been recognized as such by the local tourist industry for many years. In all, there are 72 beaches of varying sizes, some in coves, some on islands. Surfing is the main pastime, of which it is said to be capital, but there is a whole range of watersports on offer, including sailing to and around the offshore islands. The **Tropic of Capricorn** runs through the beach of Itaguá, just south of the town.

The commercial centre of Ubatuba is at the northern end of the bay by the estuary, by which the fishing boats enter and leave. A bridge crosses the estuary, giving access to the coast north of town. A small jetty with a lighthouse at the end protects the river mouth and this is a pleasant place to watch the boats come and go. The seafront, stretching south from the jetty, is built up along its length, but there are hardly any high-rise blocks. In the commercial centre are shops, banks, services, lots of restaurants (most serving pizza and fish), but few hotels. These are mainly found on the beaches north and south and can be reached from the Costamar bus terminal.

Ins and outs

The road from São Sebastião is paved, so a journey from São Paulo along the coast is possible. Ubatuba is 70 km from Paraty. There are regular buses from São Paulo, São José dos Campos, Paraibuna, Caraguatatuba, Paraty and Rio de Janeiro. The beaches are spread out over a wide area, so if you are staying in Ubatuba town and don't have a car, you will need to take one of the frequent buses. Taxis in town can be very expensive. ▶▶ *See Transport, page 84.*

The **tourist office** ① *R Guarani 465, T012-3833 9007, www.ubatuba.sp.gov.br*, is on the seafront. The area gets very crowded at carnival time as Cariocas come to escape the crowds in Rio. There is a small airport from which stunt fliers take off to wheel over the bay. In summer 10-minute panoramic flights and helicopter rides over Ubatuba are offered from US$45.

Background

This part of the coast was hotly contested between the local indigenous population and the Portuguese. The Jesuits José Anchieta and Manuel Nóbrega came to the village of Iperoig, as it was called in 1563, to put a stop to the fighting; the former was even taken hostage by the locals during the negotiations. A cross on the Praia do Cruzeiro (or Iperoig) in the centre commemorates what the town proudly claims to have been the first peace treaty on the American continent. The colonists eventually prevailed and the town of Vila Nova da Exaltação da Santa Cruz do Salvador de Ubatuba became an important port until Santos overtook it in the late 18th century. In the 20th century its development as a holiday resort was rapid, especially after 1948 when it became an Estância Balneária. The shortened name of Ubatuba derives from the Tupi-Guarani, meaning 'place of ubas', a type of tree used for making bows and canoes. Cariocas disparagingly refer to it as Uba 'chuva' – as it can rain heavily here at any time.

Sights

Ubatuba has a few historic buildings, such as the **Igreja da Matriz** on Praça da Matriz, dating back to the 18th century. It has only one tower, the old 19th-century prison, which now houses the small historical museum. Other interesting buildings include: **Cadeia Velha** on Praça Nóbrega; the 18th-century **Câmara Municipal** on Avenida Iperoig; and the **Sobrado do Porto**, the 19th-century customs house at Praça Anchieta 38, which contains **Fundart** (the Art and Culture Foundation). Mostly, though, it is a modern, functional town. In the surrounding countryside there are *fazendas* which are often incorporated into the *trilhas ecológicas* (nature trails) along the coast.

The **Projeto Tamar** ① *R Antonio Athanasio da Silva 273, Itaguá, T012-3432 6202, www.ubatuba.com.br/tamar*, is a branch of the national project which studies and preserves marine turtles. The **Aquário de Ubatuba** ① *R Guarani 859, T012-3432 1382, www.aquariodeubatuba.com.br, Fri-Wed 1000-2200*, has well-displayed Amazon and Pantanal species including caimans and piranhas.

Beaches

The only place where swimming is definitely not recommended is near the town's outflow between Praia do Cruzeiro and Praia Itaguá. The sand and water close to the jetty don't look too inviting either. The most popular beaches are **Praia Tenório**, **Praia Grande** and **Praia Toninhas** (4.5 km, 6 km and 8 km south respectively). Condominiums, apartments, hotels and *pousadas* line these beaches on both sides of the coast road. Of the municipality's 72 beaches, those to the south are the more developed although the further you go from town in either direction, the less built up they are. Boogie boards can be hired at many of the beaches, or you can buy your own in town for around US$5.

Saco da Ribeira, 13 km south, is a natural harbour that has been made into a yacht marina. Schooners leave from here for excursions to **Ilha Anchieta** (or dos Porcos), a popular four-hour trip. On the island are beaches, trails and a prison, which was in commission from 1908 to 1952. The Costamar bus from Ubatuba to Saco da Ribeira runs every half an hour (US$0.85) and will drop you at the turning by the **Restaurante Pizzeria Malibu**. It's a short walk to the docks and boatyards where an unsealed road leads to the right, through the boatyards, to a track along the shore. It ends at the **Praia da Ribeira** from where you can follow the track round a headland to the beaches of **Flamengo**, **Flamenguinho** and **Sete Fontes**. It's a pleasant stroll (about one hour to Flamengo), but there is no shade and you need to take water. Note the sign before Flamengo on one of the private properties: "*Propriedade particular. Cuidado c/o elefante!*".

Litoral Sul → *For listings, see pages 78-85.*

Unlike the Linha Verde, the Litoral Sul between Santos and Cananéia has not been continuously developed. From São Vicente to Itanhaém, the whole coast is completely built up with holiday developments, but beyond Itanhaém the road does not hug the shore and a large area has been left untouched. Some 80% of the region is now under some form of environmental protection. An organization called **SOS Mata Atlântica** ① *R Manoel da Nóbrega 456, São Paulo, www.sosmatatlantica.org.br*, aims to help preserve what is left of the coastal vegetation but is part owned by a large paper company.

Itanhaém → *Phone code: 013. Population: 72,000.*

Itanhaém lies 61 km south of Santos. Its pretty colonial church, **Sant'Ana** (1761) on Praça Narciso de Andrade, and the **Convento da Nossa Senhora da Conceição** (1699-1713, originally founded 1554), on the small hill of Morro de Itaguaçu, are reminders of the Portuguese dedication to converting the indigenous Brazilians to Catholicism. Also in the town is the **Casa de Câmara e Cadeia**, but the historic buildings are quite lost amid the modern development. The beaches here are attractive, but like those at Mongaguá and Praia Grande, several stretches are prone to pollution. Excursions can be made by boat up the **Rio Itanhaém**. Frequent buses run from Santos, an hour away. There are several good seafood restaurants along the beach, hotels and camping.

Peruíbe → *Phone code: 013. Population: 52,000.*

Some 31 km further down the coast, there are more beaches at Peruíbe, but some fall within the jurisdiction of the Estação Ecológica Juréia-Itatins (see below). While the beach culture has been well developed here with surfing, windsurfing, fishing and so on, a number of 'alternative' options have recently flourished. The climate is said to be unusually healthy owing to a high concentration of ozone, which helps to filter out harmful ultraviolet rays from the sun. UFO watchers and other esoterics claim that it is a very mystical place. Local rivers have water and black mud proven to contain medicinal properties. And the neighbouring ecological station is a major draw now that ecotourism has become big business in São Paulo state. Peruíbe's history dates back to 1530 when the village of Abarebebê was founded; about 9 km northeast of here, the ruins can be visited, with its church built of stone and shells. There is a **Feira do Artesanato** ① *Av São João, Sat and Sun 1400-0100 (1400-2300 in winter)*.

Buses connect the town with Santos, for São Paulo. For information, contact the **Secretaria de Turismo** ① *R Nilo Soares Ferreira 50, T013-3455 2070*. You may have to ask permission in the **Departamento da Cultura** ① *Centro de Convenções, Av Sã João 545, T013-3455 2232*, to visit Abarebebê and other sites. Also at this address is the **Secretaria Estadual do Meio Ambiente** ① *T013-3457 9243*, for information on the Estação Ecológico Juréia-Itatins.

Estação Ecológico Juréia-Itatins

① *Special permission is required to enter Juréia and the surrounding protected areas. They can only be visited on an organized tour with Waldhaus Ecopousada (see page 80) or Trip on Jeep (see page 61). Contact the company with at least 5 days' notice. Trip costs vary depending on duration and number of people.*

Peruíbe marks the northernmost point of the Estação Ecológico Juréia-Itatins, 820 sq km of protected *Mata Atlântica*. The four main ecosystems are *restinga*, mangrove forest, *Mata Atlântica* and the vegetation at about 900 m on the Juréia mountains. Its wildlife includes many endangered species including rare flowers and other plants. There are deer, jaguar, monkeys, dolphins, alligators and birds, including the yellow-headed woodpecker and toucans. Human occupation of the area has included sambaqui, builders, *fazendeiros* and present-day fishing communities who preserve an isolated way of life.

The ecological station was founded in 1986. Tourism is very carefully monitored and only certain areas are open to the public. Hikers can walk the 4-km **Trilha do Arpoador** and the 5-km **Trilha do Imperador**, but both need prior reservation and numbers are limited; similarly for the **Despraiado mountain bike trail**. Trips can be made, with authorization, up the **Rio Guaraú** (8 km from Peruíbe) and the **Rio Una do Prelado** (25 km from Peruíbe). Other places of interest are **Vila do Prelado**, which was a stop on the Imperial São Vicente-Iguape post route (electric light was only installed in 1995), and the **Casa da Farinha**, where manioc flour is made, 28 km from Iguape.

Iguape and Ilha Comprida → *Phone code: 013. Population: 28,000.*

At the southern end of the ecological station is the town of Iguape, founded in 1538. In the early days of its existence, ownership of the town was disputed between Spain and Portugal because it was close to the line drawn by the Pope marking their respective territories in the 'New World'. Typical of Portuguese architecture, the small **Museu Histórico e Arqueológico** ⓘ *R das Neves 45, Tue-Sun 0900-1730*, is housed in the 17th-century Casa da Oficina Real de Fundição. There is also a **Museu de Arte Sacra** ⓘ *Praça Rotary, Sat and Sun 0900-1200, 1330-1700*, in the former Igreja do Rosário. The main church, the **Basílica de Bom Jesus**, is a mid-19th-century construction. Information is available from **Prefeitura Municipal** ⓘ *R 15 de Novembro 272, T013-3841 1626*.

The main attractions for tourists are yachting, fishing and half a dozen beaches. Excursions include the ruined *fazenda* of **Itaguá**. Handicrafts include items made from wood and clay, basketware and musical instruments.

Opposite Iguape is the northern end of the **Ilha Comprida** with 86 km of beaches, some of which are disappointing. This **Área de Proteção Ambiental** is not much higher than sea level and is divided from the mainland by the Canal do Mar Pequeno. The northern end is the busiest and on the island there are hotels, a supermarket and some good restaurants; the fresh fish is excellent.

Caverns of the Vale do Ribeira and PETAR (Caverna do Santana)

This cave system, 40 km from Eldorado, west of the BR-116, forms one of the largest concentrations of caverns in the world. Among the best known is the 8-km Gruta da Tapagem or **Caverna do Diabo (Devil's Cave)** ⓘ *Mon-Fri 0800-1100, 1200-1700, Sat, Sun and holidays 0800-1700, US$2*. It is as huge as a cathedral with well-lit formations in the 600 m that are open to the public.

Some 43 km north of the Caverna do Diabo is the **Parque Estadual Turístico do Alto Ribeira (PETAR)** ⓘ *www.petaronline.com.br*, which includes three groups of caves. The Núcleo Santana, contains the Cavernas de Santana (5.6 km of subterranean passages and three levels of galleries), Morro Preto and Água Suja, plus a 3.6-km ecological trail to the waterfalls in the Rio Bethary, and the Núcleo Ouro Grosso. This section of the park is 4 km from the town of Iporanga. Iporanga is the most convenient town for visiting all the caves; it is 64 km west of Eldorado Paulista, 42 km east of Apiaí, on the SP-165, 257 km southwest of São Paulo. The third group, Núcleo Caboclos, near the town of Apiaí.

Ins and outs The nearest towns to the caves are Iporanga and Apiaí; buses run to both from the Rodoviária Barra Funda in São Paulo or you can take a bus to Registro and change there. If coming to Iporanga from Curitiba, change buses at Jacupiranga on the BR-116 for Eldorado Paulista. Most people who visit the caves use their own transport and there is little transport infrastructure for those who come without a car. However the **Pousada Quiririm** (see Sleeping, page 81), 3 km from PETAR, rents boats and can organize trips into the caves with advance notice. All trips in PETAR must be made with an accredited local guide. Tours to the region can also be organized with Trip on Jeep (see page 61).

Cananéia → *Phone code: 013.*

The 18th-century façades of the little port town of **Cananéia** stand, gradually decaying, at the heart of the wildest region in southeastern Brazil. Extensive mangrove wetlands, lowland forests and porpoise-filled estuaries surround the town on all sides. Rising up behind them are the rugged, rainforest-covered mountains of the Serra do Mar, which stretch all the way into neighbouring Paraná. The white sands of **Ilha do Cordoso** are accessible by boat, and the long broad beaches of **Boqueirão Sul**, southern Ilha Comprida, are just five minutes by ferry across the little brackish river that fronts the town.

Although this is one of the country's oldest cities (it was one of Martim Afonso de Souza's landfalls), Cananéia lacks the twee charm and tourist facilities of its cousins, Morretes to the south and Paraty to the north. The 17th-century **Igreja de São João Batista** has plants growing out of its belltower and the façades of its colonial buildings are crumbling in the humidity. The only time of year that sees many visitors is Carnaval and New Year. This is a town with an *Under the Volcano* atmosphere; it feels like the end of the line. *Pousadas* open their doors at whim. Restaurants are limited to fish, beans and rice served on plastic tables by friendly waiters. However, for those seeking out-of-the-way places, herein lies its appeal.

Ins and outs Cananéia can be easily visited on the way from São Paulo or Santos to Curitiba. At least two buses a day run to those destinations from the little *rodoviária*, a block west of the central Praça Martim Afonso de Souza.

Car and passenger ferries leave every 30 minutes from in front of the *praça* for the beach at Boqueirão Sul in southern Ilha Comprida. It takes about an hour to walk from the ferry dock to the beach. A few simple *pousadas* line the way. It is also possible to take boats all the way to Ilha do Mel in Paraná.

Ilha do Cardoso

The densely wooded Ilha do Cardoso is a Reserva Florestal e Biológica. **Marujá**, the only village on the island, is tiny and has no electricity. There are some very rustic *pousadas* and restaurants and camping is allowed at designated places, but the island is otherwise uninhabited. There are lots of idyllic beaches, where spectacled caiman can be spotted lazing on the virtually untouched white sand. The best place for surfing is **Moretinho**.

Ins and outs There are three daily ferry services from Cananéia, the journey takes four hours (the ticket office as it Rua Princesa Isabel, T013-3841 1122). Boats run tours from the docks for around US$7 per person in high season and at weekends. Launches can be hired for about US$70 for a full day at other times. Speedboats to Ilha Cardoso must be chartered in Cananéia (US$60-80 for up to five people). *Escunas* (larger boats) generally leave daily in the morning for the fishing community of Marujá and more regularly at weekends and during the high season (US$12 each way). Alternatively, drive 70 km along an unpaved road, impassable when wet, to **Ariri**, from where the island is 10 minutes by boat. Trips can also be organized with **Trip on Jeep** in São Paulo (see page 61).

The coast of São Paulo listings

For Sleeping and Eating price codes and other relevant information, see pages 10-13.

Sleeping

Santos *p66, map p67*
Discounts up to 50% during low season. There are many cheap hotels near the Orquidário Municipal a few blocks from the beach.

$$$$ Mendes Plaza, Av Floriano Peixoto 42, a block from the beach in the main shopping area, T013-3208 6400, www.mendeshoteis. com.br. A large, newly refurbished, 1970s business-orientated hotel with 2 restaurants and a rooftop pool.

$$$$ Parque Balneário Hotel, Av Ana Costa 555, Gonzaga, T013-3289 5700, www.parque balneario.com.br. The city's 5-star hotel, with full business facilities and a rooftop pool overlooking the beach. Close to the shops and restaurants. Recently renovated.

$$$ Atlântico Ville, Av Pres Wilson 1, T013-3289 4500, www.atlantico-hotel.com.br. A/c rooms in a newly renovated, well-kept 1930s hotel on the seafront. All rooms have TV; the best are in the upper floors with sea views. There's a decent business centre, sauna, bar and restaurant.

$$ Gonzaga Flats, R Jorge Tibiriçá 41, Gonzaga, T013-3289 5800, www.gonzaga flat.tur.br. Apartments in a 1990s block, all with kitchenettes and small sitting rooms with sofa beds. Space for up to 4 people.

$$ Hotel Natal, Av Mal Floriano Peixoto 104, Gonzaga T013-3284 2732, www.hotel natal.com.br. Fan-cooled or a/c apartments with or without bathrooms. Cable TV.

$$ Pousada do Marquês, Av Floriano Peixoto 202, Gonzaga, T013-3237 1951, www.pousadadomarques.hpg.ig.com.br. Very simple en suite rooms with fan and cable TV.

Camburi, Camburizinho and Maresias *p70*

$$$ Camburyzinho, Estr Camburi 200, Km 41, Camburizinho, T012-3865 2625, www.pousada camburizinho.com.br. 30 smart rooms in mock-colonial annexes gathered around a pool, with a bar and beach service.

$$ Piccolo Albergo, R Nova Iguaçu 1979, Maresias, T012-3465 6227. 5 smart chalets in a forest setting near a waterfall. With sauna and a natural swimming pool.

$$ Pousada das Praias, R Piauí 70, Camburizinho, T012-3865 1474, www.pousadadaspraias.com.br. A lovely little beachside *pousada* in tropical gardens, with annexes of thatched-roof wooden rooms with large glass windows and terraces overlooking a pool and sauna. The *pousada* contributes part of its profits to the local community.

São Sebastião *p70*
The city itself is not particularly desirable so only stay here if you have to, otherwise it's best to head for Ilhabela. There are a few cheap places near the main *praça* and *rodoviária*.

$$ Roma, Praça João Fernandes 174, T012-3892 1016, www.hotelroma.tur.br. Simple but well-maintained rooms around a fig-tree filled courtyard. The simplest are a little scruffy. Includes breakfast.

Camping
Camping do Barraqueçaba Bar de Mar de Lucas, near the beach about 6 km south of São Sebastião. Hot showers, English spoken, cabins available. Recommended.

Ilhabela *p71*
There are a number of moderate and cheap hotels on the road to the left of the ferry.

$$$$ Barulho d'Agua, R Manoel Pombo 250, Curral, Km 14, T012-3894 2021, www.barulho dagua.com.br. Intimate little cabins with thatched roofs and rustic, chunky wood furniture set in rainforest next to a clear river. Very romantic and with a good restaurant.

$$$$ Maison Joly, R Antonio Lisboa Alves 278, Morro do Cantagalo, T012-3896 1201, www.maisonjoly.com.br. Exquisite little *pousada* perfect for couples. Each cabin is tastefully decorated in its own style and has a wonderful view out over the bay. Great restaurant and pool. Private, intimate and quiet. No children allowed.

$$$ Ilhabela, Av Pedro Paulo de Morais 151, Saco da Capela. T012-3896 1083, www.hotel ilhabela.com.br. One of the larger *pousadas*, orientated to families and with a well-equipped but small gym, pool, restaurant and bar and good breakfast. Recommended.

$$$ Porto Pousada Saco da Capela, R Itapema 167, T012-3896 8020, www.sacodacapela.com.br. 18 carefully decorated cabins set in a rocky forest garden on a steep hill. Good pool and breakfast.

$$ Canto Bravo, Praia do Bonete, T012-9766 0478, www.pousadacantobravo.com.br. Set on a secluded beach 1½ hrs' walk (or 20-min boat ride) from Ponta de Sepituba. Modest and elegantly decorated cabins and excellent simple breakfast and lunch (included in the price).

$$ Ilhabela, R Benedito Serafim Sampaio 371, Pereque, T012-3896 2725, www.bonnsventos hostel.com.br. A well-kept and well-run mock-colonial hostel with terracotta tiled roofs and solid wooden and whicker furniture in smart, airy public areas. Dorms are stark and simple – with little more than beds and lockers. Suites are more spacious and brighter, with metal tables outside and en suite bathrooms. The hostel has a pool, a large garden and sits a short walk from the beach.

$$ Pousada dos Hibiscos, Av Pedro Paulo de Morais 714, T012-3896 1375, www.pousada doshibiscos.com.br. Little group of cabins set around a pool with a sauna, gym and bar. Nice atmosphere. Recommended.

$$ Tamara, R Jacob Eduardo Toedtli 163, Itaquanduba, T012-3896 2543, www.pousada- tamara.com.br. 17 *cabañas* with a/c around a small pool.

$$ Vila das Pedra, R Antenor Custodio da Silva 46, Cocaia, T012-3896 2433, www.viladas pedras.com.br. 11 chalets in a forest garden. Tastefully decorated and a very nice pool.

Camping

In addition to **Pedra do Sino**, T012-3896 1266, www.campingpedradosino.com.br, there are campsites at **Perequê**, T011-7202 2840, www.ilhabela.com/camping, near the ferry dock, and at **Praia Grande**, T012-3894 1506, www.cantogrande.com.br, a further 11 km south.

Ubatuba *p73*

Very cheap accommodation is hard to come by and at all holiday times no hotel charges less than US$30.

$$ São Charbel, Praça Nóbrega 280, T012-3832 1090, www.saocharbel.com.br. Plain white a/c rooms with floor tiles, double beds with fitted bedside tables and Brazilian TV. The hotel sits on the busy main square. The advertised rooftop 'pool' is, in reality, a tiny plunge pool.

$$ São Nicolau, R Conceição 213, T012-3832 5007, www.hotelsaonicolau.com.br. Very simple a/c rooms sitting over a colourful restaurant, a 3-min walk from the bus station. The *pousada* is convenient for the town beach restaurants and services. Friendly and well looked after, with a good breakfast.

$$ Xaréu, R Jordão Homem da Costa 413, T012- 3832 1525, www.hotelxareu batuba.com.br. 3-min walk from the bus station, convenient for the town beach restaurants and services. Pretty rooms with wrought-iron balconies in a pleasant garden area. Good value, excellent breakfast.

Beach hotels

$$$$ Recanto das Toninhas, Praia das Toninhas, T012-3842 1410, www.toninhas.com.br. Part of the **Roteiros de Charme** group (see page 11). Elegant *cabañas* and suites of rooms in a large thatched-rofed building. The best with have sea views and are set around a very pretty pool with a full range of services and activities, including a sauna, restaurant, bar, tennis court and excursions.

$$$ Refúgio do Corsário, Baia Fortaleza, 25 km south of Ubatuba, T012-3443 9148, www.corsario.com.br. A clean, quiet hotel on the waterfront with a large pool set on a palm-shaded lawn overlooking the ocean. Prices are for full board and the hotel offers a range of activities including sailing and swimming. Very relaxing.

$$$ Saveiros, R Laranjeira 227, Praia do Lázaro, 14 km from town, T012-3842 0172, www.hotel saveiros.com.br. Pretty little *pousada* with a pool and a decent restaurant. English spoken.

$$$ Solar das Águas Cantantes, Estr Saco da Ribeira 253, Praia do Lázaro, Km 14, T012-3842 0178, www.solardasaguascantantes.com.br. A mock-Portuguese colonial house replete with *azulejos* and set in a shady tropical garden. The restaurant is one of the best on the São Paulo coast and serves excellent seafood and Bahian dishes.

$$ Rosa Penteado, Av Beira-Mar 183, Praia de Picinguaba, T012-3836 9119, www.pousadarosapicinguaba.com.br. 4 pretty beachside *cabañas* decorated with paintings and objects made by the owner. The price includes a very good breakfast and dinner.

$ Tribo Hostel, R Amoreira 71, Praia do Lázaro, 14 km from Ubatuba, T012-3432 0585, www.ubatubahostel.com. Great value hostel on one of the prettiest beaches in Ubatuba. Simple tiled dorms and doubles, all fan-cooled and with shared bathrooms. The hostel has a pool and a simple restaurant and attracts a busy party crowd at weekends, but is quiet from Sun to Thu night. Details on how to get to the hostel from Ubatuba town on the website.

Camping

Be careful camping around Ubatuba, especially on weekends. Robbery and assault are increasingly common.

Camping Clube do Brasil, Lagoinha, 25 km from town, T012-3443 1536, www.campingclube.com.br; also at Praia Perequê-Açu, 2 km north, T012-3432 1682. There are about 8 other sites in the vicinity.

Peruíbe *p75*

$$$ Piero Al Mare, R Indianópolis 20, Praia Orla dos Coqueiros, T013-458 2603. Modest, plain rooms with breakfast and a restaurant.

$$ Vila Real, Av Anchieta 6625, T013-3458 2797. Basic, well looked after with good staff.

$$ Waldhaus Ecopousada Casa da Floresta, R Gaviota 1201, Praia do Guaraú, T013-3522 4122, www.jureiaecoadventure.com.br. A big, brightly coloured mock-German chalet in glorious surrounds – set in a sloth and hummingbird-filled tropical garden on a cape with sweeping views over the beach to the forests of Juréia. Rooms are plain but comfortable – decked out in polished wood and with doubles and sofa beds and the *pousada* offer trips into Juréia by foot, jeep or canoe. Money from the hotel goes towards community projects.

Iguape and Ilha Comprida *p76*

The northern part of Ilha Comprida is reached from Iguape. The southern part of Ilha Comprida is closer to Cananéia. There are hotels in the southern end too, reachable from Cananeia. All those listed here are in Iguape.

$$ Silvi, R Ana Cândida Sandoval Trigo 515, Iguape, T013-3841 1421, silvihotel.com.br. Very simple rooms in a low-rise concrete comples in the town. Staff are friendly and see very few foreigners.

$$ Solar Colonial Pousada, Praça da Basilica 30, Iguape, T013-3841 1591. A range of rooms in a converted 19th-century house.

Camping

There is a campsite at **Praia da Barra da Ribeira**, 20 km north, and wild camping is possible at **Praia de Juréia**, the gateway to the ecological station.

Caverns of the Vale do Ribeiro *p76*

$$ Pousada das Cavernas, Iporanga, T015-3556 1168 or T011-3543 3082, www.pousadadascavernas.com.br. Pleasant, simple with breakfast.

$$ Pousada Quiririm, Rodovia Antonio Honório da Silva, Km 156, 6 Bairro da Serra, Iporanga, www.pousadadoquiririm.com.br. Pretty litte *pousada* with chalets set in a sub-tropical garden overlooking the forest. Organizes trips to the caves. Full board. Book ahead, especially at weekends.

$ Pousada Rancho da Serra, Iporanga, T015-3556 1168 or T011-3588 2011, www.ranchodaserra.com.br. Friendly staff organize trips into PETAR. Rooms are very simple.

Cananéia *p77*

There are a few cheap hotels in Cananéia town and other more expensive options across the water (2 mins on ferry and about 30-min walk) on the southern end of Ilha Comprida (see page 76). R Tristã Lobo lies a few blocks inland from the *praça* and runs parallel to the shoreline.

$$ Pousada do Pedrinho, R Tristão Lobo 49, Cananéia historical centre, T013-3851 1368. Simple, a/c motel-like rooms with tiled floors and TVs and a small restaurant. No sign outside the hotel. R Tristão Lobo lies 2 blocks inland from the main *praça*.

$ Villa (São João Baptysta) de Cananea, R Tristã Lobo 289, T013-3851 3367, www.pousadavilladecananea.com.br. A small, charming family *pousada* in a converted 18th-century house. Simple but welcoming with chunky faux-antique furniture, friendly staff and a big breakfast. The hotel can organize fishing trips and excursions.

Ilha do Cardoso *p77*

$$ Pousada do Sossego, Praia do Marujá, Ilha do Cardoso, T013-3852 1141, www.cananet.com.br/sossego. Simple rooms in shacks right on a pristine, lonely stretch of beach. They can organize trail walks, boat trips and fishing.

$$ Pousada Ilha do Cardoso, Praia do Marujá, Ilha do Cardoso, T013-3852 1613. A little concrete house near the beach and on the edge of the fishing village, with terraces and breakfast included.

Eating

Santos *p66, map p67*

¶¶ Old Harbour, Av Ana Costa 555, in the Parque Balneário Hotel, T013-3289 5700. Traditional Brazilian fare with daily lunch buffets and a hearty *feijoada* on Sat lunch.

¶¶ Pier One, Av Almirante Saldanha da Gama, Ponta da Praia. Good evening option in a restaurant perched over the water next to the Ponte Edgard Perdigao bridge. Very good *meca santista* – a local fish speciality served with banana, manioc flour and bacon – and live music at weekends.

¶¶ WTC, R 15 de Novembro 111/113, Centro Histórico, T013-3219 7175. A business man's club housed in a handsome 19th-century building. Popular with local bigwigs. One of the best restaurants in the city with a Mediterranean-influenced menu.

¶¶-¶ Point 44, R Jorge Tibiriçá 44. Great lunchtime buffet with enormous choice of *churrascaria*, in a large bustling dining room. Bar snack menu, live music Tue-Sat evening and dancing on Tue, Thu and Sat.

¶ Café Paulista, Praça Rui Barbosa 8 at R do Comércio, Centro Histórico, T013-3219 5550. A Santos institution. Founded in 1911 by Italians, this place has been serving great

Portuguese dishes such as *bacalhau*, and bar snacks (such as *empada camarão*), and coffee.

Camburi, Camburizinho and Maresias *p70*

There are numerous cheap and mid-range restaurants with bars and nightclubs along the São Sebastião coast and some excellent restaurants around Camburizinho.

¥¥¥ Acqua, R Estr. Do Camburi 2000, Camburizinho, T012-3865 1866. Superb food with a view – out over Camburi and Praia de Baleia beach. Come for a sunset cocktail and then dine by candlelight.

¥¥¥ Manacá, R do Manacá, Camburizinho, T012-3865 1566. Closed Mon and Wed. One of the best restaurants on the São Paulo coast and one of the best in the state, using French cooking techniques with Brazilian, Asian and seafood ingredients. Specialities include sole in orange and ginger sauce, puréed potato and wasabi. Very romantic setting, in a rainforest garden reached by a candlelit boardwalk. Come for dinner. Worth a special trip.

São Sebastião *p70*

¥ São Sebastião bar and restaurant, Praça Major João Fernades 278, diagonally opposite the Igreja Matriz, T012-3892 4100. Generous *pratos feitos*, fish and chicken and great juices. Very good value.

Ilhabela *p71*

There are cheap places in the town, including a decent *padaria* (bakery) and snack bars.

¥¥¥ Pizzabela, Hotel Ilha Deck, Av Alm Tamandaré 805, Itaguassu, T012-3896 1489. Paulistanos consider their pizza the best in the world. This is one of the few restaurants outside the city serving pizza, São Paulo-style. Expect lots of cheese. Nice surrounds.

¥¥¥ Viana, Av Leonardo Reale 1560, Praia do Viana, T012-3896 1089. The best and most expensive restaurant on the island, with excellent seafood and light Italian dishes. Good wine list. Book ahead.

Ubatuba *p73*

There is a string of mid-range restaurants along the seafront on Av Iperoig, as far as the roundabout by the airport.

¥¥¥ Giorgio, Av Leovigildo Dias Vieira 248, Itaguá. Sophisticated Italian restaurant and bar.

¥¥¥ Solar das Águas Cantantes, (see Sleeping). Very good seafood and Bahian restaurant in elegant surrounds.

¥¥ Pizzeria São Paulo, Praça da Paz de Iperoig 26. Undeniably chic gourmet pizzeria in beautifully restored building. Owned by a young lawyer who brings the authentic Italian ingredients for the gorgeous pizzas from São Paulo every weekend.

¥¥ Senzala, Av Iperoig. Established 30 years ago, this Italian has a lovely atmosphere. Don't miss the seafood spaghetti. Recommended.

¥ Armazém da Praia, R Cel Ernesto de Oliveira 149, opposite the post office. Open for lunch only. Pretty, family-run self-service.

¥ Sérgio, R Prof Thomaz Galhardo 404. Open for dinner, weekends only. Serving ice-cream, pizza and, at weekends, *feijoada*.

⦿ Festivals and events

Santos *p66, map p67*

Throughout the summer there are many cultural, educational and sporting events.
26 Jan Foundation of Santos.
Mar/Apr Good Fri.
Jun Corpus Christi; Festejos Juninos.
8 Sep Nossa Senhora de Monte Serrat.

São Sebastião *p70*

20 Jan Festival of the Patron Saint, featuring *congadas*, a song and dance derived from slaves from the Congo.

Ilhabela *p71*

There are sailing weeks and fishing contests throughout the year; dates change annually.
Feb Carnaval.
May Ilhabela is rich in folklore and legends.

The biggest rodeo in the world

The world's biggest annual rodeo, the Festa do Peão Boiadeiro, is held during the third week in August in Barretos, some 115 km northwest of Ribeirão Preto. The town is completely taken over as up to a million fans come to watch the horsemanship, enjoy the concerts, eat, drink and shop in what has become the epitome of Brazilian cowboy culture. There are over 1000 rodeos a year in Brazil, but this is the ultimate. The stadium, which has a capacity for 35,000 people, was designed by Oscar Niemeyer and the wind funnels through the middle, cool the competitors and the spectators. Since the 1950s, when Barretos' rodeo began, the event grew slowly until the mid-1980s when it really took off.

Tours from the UK are run by **Last Frontiers**, www.lastfrontiers.co.uk.

Its version of *congada* is famous, particularly at the **Festival of São Benedito**.
28 Jun São Pedro, with a maritime procession.
1st week of Jul Santa Verônica in Bonete.
Sep The town's anniversary.

Ubatuba *p73*
Feb Carnaval.
End Jun São Pedro.
Jul Festa do Divino Espírito Santo.
Sep Ubatuba is known for its handicrafts (carved wood, basketware) and it holds an annual **Festa da Cultura Popular**.
28 Oct Ubatuba's anniversary.

Peruíbe *p75*
18 Feb Founding of Peruíbe.
Jun Festival do Inverno.
Oct Mês das Missões.

Iguape and Ilha Comprida *p76*
Throughout the year there are various sporting and cultural events.
Jan/Feb Summer festival in Iguape.
Feb Carnaval on Ilha Comprida.
Mar/Apr Semana Santa.
Jun Corpus Christi.
Aug The month of the pilgrimage of **Senhor Bom Jesus de Iguape**.
3 Dec Iguape's anniversary.

▲ Activities and tours

Caverns of the Vale do Ribeiro *p76*
Tour operators
Agência de Monitores Parque Aventuras, Bairro da Serra, Iporanga, T015-3556 1485, www.parqueaventuras.com.br. Trips to the caves, waterfalls and forests around PETAR and light adventure activities including rapelling. Come during the week. At weekends big groups from São Paulo make things noisy and boyish.
Trip on Jeep, see page 61. Run trips to wildlife destinations along the São Paulo coast, including Jureia and PETAR.

⊖ Transport

Santos *p66, map p67*
Bus To **São Vicente**, US$0.90. For most suburbs buses leave from Praça Mauá, in the centre of the city. Heading south, several daily buses connect Santos to **Peruíbe**, **Iguape** and **Cananeia** for **Ilha Comprida** and **Ilha do Cardoso**.

There are buses to **São Paulo** (50 mins, US$5) approximately every 15 mins, from the *rodoviária* near the city centre, José Menino or Ponta da Praia (opposite the ferry to Guarujá). Note that the 2 highways between São Paulo and Santos are sometimes very crowded, especially at rush hours and weekends. To **Guarulhos/**

Cumbica airport, Expresso Brasileiro at 0600, 1330, 1830, return 0550, 0930, 1240, 1810, US$20, allow plenty of time as the bus goes through Guarulhos, 3 hrs. **TransLitoral** from Santos to **Congonhas airport** then to Guarulhos/Cumbica, 4 daily, US$12, 2 hrs. To **Rio de Janeiro**, Normandy, several daily, 7½ hrs, US$40. To Rio along the coast road is via **São Sebastião** (US$10, change buses if necessary), **Caraguatatuba** and **Ubatuba**.

Taxi All taxis have meters. The fare from Gonzaga to the bus station is about US$15. Cooper Rádio táxi, T013-3232 7177.

São Sebastião *p70*
Bus 2 buses a day to **Rio de Janeiro** with Normandy, 0830 and 2300 (plus 1630 on Fri and Sun), can be heavily booked in advance, US$30 (US$10 from Paraty) 6½ hrs; 12 a day to **Santos**, via Guarujá, 4 hrs, US$11; 11 buses a day also to **São Paulo**, US$15, which run inland via **São José dos Campos**, unless you ask for the service via **Bertioga**, only 2 a day. Other buses run along the coast via **Maresias**, **Camburi** or north through **Ubatuba**. Last bus leaves at 2200.

Ferry Free ferry to **Ilhabela** for foot passengers, see below.

Ilhabela *p71*
Bus A bus runs along the coastal strip facing the mainland. **Litorânea** runs buses from Ilhabela town through to **São Paulo** (office at R Dr Carvalho 136) but it is easiest to reach the island by taking a bus from São Paulo to São Sebastião across the water and then the ferry across to Ilhabela.

Ferry The 15- to 20-min ferry to **São Sebastião** runs non-stop day and night. Free for foot passengers; cars cost US$1 weekdays, US$10 at weekends.

Ubatuba *p73*
Bus There are 3 bus terminals.
Rodoviária Costamar, R Hans Staden and R Conceição, serves all local destinations.

The *rodoviária* at R Prof Thomaz Galhardo 513, for São José buses to **Paraty**, US$2.25, some Normandy services to **Rio de Janeiro**, US$9 and some Itapemirim buses.

Rodoviária Litorânea is the main bus station. To get there, go up Conceição for 8 blocks from Praça 13 de Maio, turn right on R Rio Grande do Sul, then left into R Dra Maria V Jean. Buses go to **São Paulo**, 3½ hrs, frequent, US$8, **São José dos Campos**, US$6, **Paraibuna**, US$5, **Caraguatatuba**, US$2.

Iguape and Ilha Comprida *p76*
Bus Buses run from Iguape to **São Paulo**, **Santos** or **Curitiba**, changing at Registro.

Ferry A continuous ferry service runs from Iguape to Ilha Comprida (free but small charge for cars); buses run until 1900 from the ferry stop to the beaches. From Iguape it is possible to take a boat trip down the coast to **Cananéia** and **Ariri**. Tickets and information from Dpto Hidroviário do Estado, R Major Moutinho 198, Iguape, T013-3841 1122. It is a beautiful trip, passing between the island and the mainland.

Caverns of the Vale do Ribeiro *p76*
Bus Buses from Apiaí run to the Barra Funda *rodoviária* in **São Paulo**, US$22. If heading to **Curitiba**, take the bus from Iporanga to Jacupiranga on the BR-116 and change.

Cananéia and Ilha do Cardoso *p77*
Bus Buses run twice daily from Cananéia to **São Paulo** (Barra Funda). Alternatively go via **Registro** (from where there are buses hourly to Barra Funda).

Directory

Santos *p66, map p67*
Banks Open 1000-1730. ATMs in Santos are very unreliable and often out of order. Visa ATMs at **Banco do Brasil**, R 15 de Novembro 195, Centro and Av Ana Costa, Gonzaga. Many others. **Embassies and consulates** France, R General Câmara 12, sala 51, T013-3219 5161. **Germany**, R Frei Gaspar 22, 10th floor, T013-3219 5092. **UK**, R Tuiuti 58, 2nd floor, T013-3219 6622.
Immigration Polícia Federal, Praça da República. **Internet** F hop, Shopping Parque Balneário. US$3 per hr. **Laundry** Av Mcal Floriano Peixoto 120, Gonzaga, self-service, wash and dry US$5. **Medical services** Ana Costa, R Pedro Américo 42, Campo Grande, T013-3222 9000; **Santa Casa de Misericórdia**, Av Dr Cláudio Luiz da Costa 50, Jabaquara, T013-3234 7575. **Post office** R Cidade de Toledo 41, Centro and at R Tolentino Filgueiras 70, Gonzaga. **Telephone** R Galeão Carvalhal 45, Gonzaga.

Ilhabela *p71*
Banks Bradesco, Praça Col Julião M Negrão 29 in Vila Ilhabela.

Ubatuba *p73*
Banks There is a **Banco 24 Horas** next to the tourist office and an **HSBC** ATM at 85 R Conceição. The **Banco do Brasil** in Praça Nóbrega does not have ATMs. **Internet** Chat and Bar, upper floor of Ubatuba Shopping. US$3 per hr, Mon-Sat 1100-2000. **Post office** R Dona Maria Alves between Hans Staden and R Col Dominicano.
Telephone On Galhardo, close to Sérgio restaurant.

Index

A
accommodation 10
air 6
ATMs 15

B
bandeirantes 24
Banespa Tower 29
Boqueirão Sul 77
bus 7
business hours 16

C
cachaça 12
Camburi 70
camping 10
Cananéia 77
churrasco 12
consulates 14
cost of travelling 15
credit cards 16
currency 15

D
drinking 12

E
eating 12
electricity 14
embassies 14
emergency 14
Estação Ecológico Juréia-Itatins 75

F
feijoada 12
Flamengo 74
Flamenguinho 74
food 12

G
Gonzaga 66
Gonzaguinha 70

H
health 14
homestays 11
hotels 10

I
Iguape 76
Ilha Anchieta 74
Ilha Comprida 76
Ilha de São Sebastião 71
Ilha do Cardoso 77
Ilha Porchat 70
Ilhabela 71
immigration 18
Interlagos 42
Itanhaém 75
Itaquitanduva 70
Itararé 70

L
Litoral Norte 70
Litoral Sul 74

M
Maresias 70
Marujá 77
mêtro 7
money 15
Monte Serrat 69
Moretinho 77

O
opening hours 16

P
Paranapiacaba 42
Parque Burle Marx 41
Pelé 69
Peruíbe 75
police 17
price codes 11

R
restaurant price codes 11
restaurants 12
rodeo 83
rodízios 12

S
Saco da Ribeira 74
safety 16
Santos 66
São Paulo 20
    Agua Branca 32
    arriving at night 21
    Avenida Paulista 32
    Banespa Tower 29
    Barra Funda 32
    botanic gardens 39
    cathedral 25
    centro histórico 25
    Cidade Universitária 40
    Ipiranga 40
    Itaim 39, 46
    Jardins 34
    Liberdade 36
    listings 43
    Luz 30
    Mosteiro do São Bento 28
    Paraíso 37
    Praça da República 29
    Praça da Sé 25
    Vila Madalena 36
    Vila Mariana 37
São Sebastião 70
São Vicente 66
Sete Fontes 74
sleeping 10

T
taxis 9
time 17
tipping 17
train 7
tourist information 17
Tropic of Capricorn 73

U
Ubatuba 73

V
Vale do Ribeiro caves 76
visas 18
voltage 14

W
weights and measures 18

Titles available in the Footprint *Focus* range

Latin America	UK RRP	US RRP
Bahia & Salvador	£7.99	$11.95
Buenos Aires & Pampas	£7.99	$11.95
Costa Rica	£8.99	$12.95
Cuzco, La Paz & Lake Titicaca	£8.99	$12.95
El Salvador	£5.99	$8.95
Guadalajara & Pacific Coast	£6.99	$9.95
Guatemala	£8.99	$12.95
Guyana, Guyane & Suriname	£5.99	$8.95
Havana	£6.99	$9.95
Honduras	£7.99	$11.95
Nicaragua	£7.99	$11.95
Paraguay	£5.99	$8.95
Quito & Galápagos Islands	£7.99	$11.95
Recife & Northeast Brazil	£7.99	$11.95
Rio de Janeiro	£8.99	$12.95
São Paulo	£5.99	$8.95
Uruguay	£6.99	$9.95
Venezuela	£8.99	$12.95
Yucatán Peninsula	£6.99	$9.95

Asia	UK RRP	US RRP
Angkor Wat	£5.99	$8.95
Bali & Lombok	£8.99	$12.95
Chennai & Tamil Nadu	£8.99	$12.95
Chiang Mai & Northern Thailand	£7.99	$11.95
Goa	£6.99	$9.95
Hanoi & Northern Vietnam	£8.99	$12.95
Ho Chi Minh City & Mekong Delta	£7.99	$11.95
Java	£7.99	$11.95
Kerala	£7.99	$11.95
Kolkata & West Bengal	£5.99	$8.95
Mumbai & Gujarat	£8.99	$12.95

Africa	UK RRP	US RRP
Beirut	£6.99	$9.95
Damascus	£5.99	$8.95
Durban & KwaZulu Natal	£8.99	$12.95
Fès & Northern Morocco	£8.99	$12.95
Jerusalem	£8.99	$12.95
Johannesburg & Kruger National Park	£7.99	$11.95
Kenya's beaches	£8.99	$12.95
Kilimanjaro & Northern Tanzania	£8.99	$12.95
Zanzibar & Pemba	£7.99	$11.95

Europe	UK RRP	US RRP
Bilbao & Basque Region	£6.99	$9.95
Granada & Sierra Nevada	£6.99	$9.95
Málaga	£5.99	$8.95
Orkney & Shetland Islands	£5.99	$8.95
Skye & Outer Hebrides	£6.99	$9.95

North America	UK RRP	US RRP
Vancouver & Rockies	£8.99	$12.95

Australasia	UK RRP	US RRP
Brisbane & Queensland	£8.99	$12.95
Perth	£7.99	$11.95

For the latest books, e-books and smart phone app releases, and a wealth of travel information, visit us at:
www.footprinttravelguides.com.

footprinttravelguides.com

Join us on facebook for the latest travel news, product releases, offers and amazing competitions: www.facebook.com/footprintbooks.com.